William Hughes

Makers
of the
Modern
World

William Hughes
Australia
Carl Bridge

HH
HAUS HISTORIES

First published in Great Britain in 2011 by
Haus Publishing Ltd
70 Cadogan Place
London SW1X 9AH
www.hauspublishing.com

Copyright © Carl Bridge, 2011

The moral right of the author has been asserted

A CIP catalogue record for this book
is available from the British Library

ISBN 978-1-905791-90-3

Series design by Susan Buchanan
Typeset in Sabon by MacGuru Ltd
Printed in Dubai by Oriental Press

Contents

Acknowledgements

I wish to record my thanks to the Australian Prime Ministers Centre, Canberra, for granting me a fellowship in 2009 and to King's College London for the study leave which made the research for this book possible. I am also grateful to my friends and colleagues, Scott Bennett, Frank Bongiorno, John Connor, Michael Cook, David Lee, Richard Murison and Kerry Sanderson, for their comments on early drafts, and to seminars at the APMC and at the Menzies Centre for Australian Studies, King's College London, for constructive criticism. My children, Andrew, Wendy and Harry, were, as ever, a constant source of encouragement and strength, and I dedicate this work to them.

Carl Bridge
London
July 2010

Introduction

The most recent biographies of William Morris 'Billy' Hughes, Australia's Prime Minister during the turbulent days of the First World War, are now 30 years old. One is an essay on his rhetoric; one a study of how he worked the Labor Party and trades union machines; and the third, his authorised biography, is comprehensive and an excellent piece of work but now dated.[1] All were written mainly for the domestic Australian market and pay insufficient attention to the international and Imperial contexts in which Hughes functioned and imagined himself. The two books on Hughes at Versailles are carefully researched and perceptive but suffer from nationalistic blinkers. A recently completed, epic two-volume study of Australian defence and diplomacy in the years before, during and immediately after the First World War, is much better in this regard, but it does not focus consistently on Hughes.[2] The most recent study of Anglo-Australian relations during the War is strong on the military side but its discussion of Versailles is curiously perfunctory and inconsequential.[3] It is more than time for a re-appraisal of the career of Billy Hughes.

My study aims to set Hughes firmly in his wider context, as

a prominent figure in the far-flung British diaspora that characterised the British Empire at its height, the phenomenon historians are now describing as 'the British World'.[4] It will show how Hughes operated as a quintessentially 'independent Australian Briton' of his time. In order to do so, it will link the local, national and international dimensions of his activities and demonstrate the ways in which each influenced – indeed, at key moments, leveraged – the others. Hughes's enemies demonised him as a 'Labor rat' who betrayed his party; his friends saw him as the 'Little Digger' who was his country's political saviour during its greatest crisis. His finest hour was at the Paris Peace Conference in 1919, when, as Australia's representative, he defied the odds to secure vital concessions for his country and Empire. He was arguably Australia's most significant politician of the 20th century and an Imperial figure of the first rank.

William Hughes with his wife Mary and an Australian delegation at Euston
Station in 1915.

I

The Life and the Land

1
New South Welshman, 1862–1901

Like his illustrious British contemporary, David Lloyd George, William Morris Hughes was a Welshman who happened to be born in England, in his case in London; unlike Lloyd George, Hughes made his career as a New South Welshman, as an Australian Briton. Born on 25 September 1862 in the London working-class suburb of Pimlico, which acted as a buffer between moneyed Belgravia and the 'Devil's Acre' and other Westminster slums, William, 'Little Willy', Will or Billy as he became known, was the only child of a Welsh-speaking carpenter and his English-speaking Welsh wife. His father, who was originally from Holyhead in Anglesey, north Wales, worked maintaining the Houses of Parliament, was a deacon in his local Particular Baptist Church, and a pillar of respectable working class Toryism. His mother, who was Anglican, worked in service. Her family had for generations owned and worked a small farm at Llansantffraid, also in north Wales just 3 miles across the border with England. Hughes was thus a cultural hybrid, truly British: a Cockney Welshman, relatively anglicised and the result of two internal migrations from the Welsh countryside to the English and Imperial metropolis.

Will Hughes spent his first 22 years in state schools in inner London and on the north Welsh borders. His mother died when he was six years old and he went to live with his father's sister who ran a substantial boarding house in the Welsh holiday town of Llandudno, where he attended the local grammar school. Here he was taught well in English but also picked up a smattering of colloquial Welsh. Despite his small frame (he grew to a very spare, though wiry, 5 feet 5 inches) and chronic dyspepsia, which bedevilled him all his life, he became a good sportsman as a runner and with his fists, and a champion at marbles.

Aged nearly 12, Will moved back to London and attended St Stephen's Grammar School in Pimlico, where two years later he became a pupil teacher for five years. There he was inspired by the great Liberal intellectual Matthew Arnold, who inspected the school and presented him with a prize of the complete works of Shakespeare, probably for his ability at reading aloud. Perhaps it was also Arnold who later inspired in him the ideal that an enlightened elite should govern the state for the benefit of all.[1] At St Stephen's Hughes read widely, learned French well, played cricket, rang the church bells and later remembered leading boisterous 'hit-and-run' raids on the local Wesleyan school when he would guard his shins for the fray by cramming exercise books into his socks.[2] But among the most important skills learned there would have been how to keep the attention of very large classes of potentially unruly pupils.

When he finished his apprenticeship and could afford it, he joined a volunteer battalion of the Royal Fusiliers. Unable or unwilling to secure a permanent teaching post, shunning the offer of a clerk's stool in Coutts' Bank and lured by adventure, he and a friend took advantage of one of the great, readily accessible human highways of the British world and migrated to Queensland on a colonial government-assisted passage in October 1884.

The Australia to which Hughes emigrated – the six separate Australian colonies of New South Wales, Victoria, South Australia, Western Australia, Tasmania and Queensland – was one of a number of 'neo-Britains', countries of British settlement spread across the globe, alongside Canada, Newfoundland and New Zealand. These were thrusting, raw, new frontier societies, with a preponderance of men and youth, politically advanced and liberal, yet parts of 'Greater Britain' none the less. Among them, the Australian colonies first introduced the secret ballot, male then universal suffrage, payment of MPs, 'secular, compulsory and free' primary education, industrial arbitration, an eight-hour day for skilled workers, and the world's first Labor government. All this occurred a generation and more in advance of the Mother Country.

The colonists across the diaspora saw themselves as building modern and better Britains. The telephone, tramway, bicycle and electric light arrived in Australia in the 1880s. 'Marvellous Melbourne', built on the foundations of the mid-century gold rushes, saw itself as the second city of the Empire after London. The Australian economy rode on the sheep's back (wool being the principal export); but beef, wheat and minerals (gold, copper, silver, lead and zinc) were also significant. The limits of agrarian settlement had been reached in the 1870s in most colonies but California-style irrigation schemes were promising more intensive farming along the rivers. The infrastructure was growing apace; and with the railway and telegraph, 'the mighty bush ... was tethered to the world'.[3] In 1875 there were only 1,000 miles of track and by 1891 there were 10,000. An era ended in 1880 when

Ned Kelly, the last great bushranger or outlaw, was captured at Glenrowan in rural Victoria with the aid of the steam train and the electric telegraph. A year earlier, the first cargo of frozen beef had been shipped from Sydney to London on the *Strathleven*. The era of the Imperial breakfast table had arrived.

The Australian population was 2.25 million in 1881, with a third living in towns and cities and fuelling a building boom. Literacy was virtually universal and women had been admitted to the University of Adelaide. Judged by meat consumption, Australians at that time had the highest standard of living in the world. The visiting British Fabian socialist, Beatrice Webb, remarked on the colonials' 'vulgarity and a rather gross materialism'[4] but they preferred to think of themselves as living in a 'workingman's paradise'.[5] Although in its peak years since the gold rushes of the 1850s government-assisted migration had added 38,054 in 1883 and 23,633 in 1884 (of whom Hughes was one), by this time nearly two-thirds of the people were Australian-born.[6] An Australian Natives' Association, for white colonists, had been formed in 1871 and, to mark their Australian-ness, they celebrated Wattle Day, when the first native flowers bloomed after winter, and used three Aboriginal 'cooees', or bush calls, instead of three cheers at meetings. The Heidelberg School of Australian Impressionists, among whose leading lights were Tom Roberts, Frederick McCubbin, Arthur Streeton and Charles Conder, were about to paint 'authentic' Australian landscapes; and a distinctive Australian literature was about to emerge featuring the bush authors Henry Lawson, 'Banjo' Paterson, Steele Rudd and Joseph Furphy. An Australian XI won the first 'Ashes' cricket series against England in 1882, beating the English at their own game.

Yet this burgeoning nationalism was also clothed in Imperial garb. The colonies fell over each other to offer a contingent to help avenge General Gordon in the Sudan in 1885 – New South Wales won – and they were very proud that the British Royal Navy, the world's strongest, guarded their coastline from its 'Australian Station' in Sydney Harbour. Many of the leading politicians, lawyers and businessmen aspired to or possessed Imperial knighthoods. Australians may have been radical and a little raffish, but they were also more literate, well-fed and 'respectable' than those they left behind in Europe.

Like hundreds of thousands before and after him, Will (soon to be rechristened Billy) Hughes arrived in Queensland anxious to put his foot on the first rung of the ladder of colonial success in this land of opportunities. He soon learnt it was a land prone not only to droughts and floods but to violent booms and busts in the labour market. In the previous 30 years, 29 million acres of land had been sold but, in this driest of continents, only half a million had been cultivated; 'wool kings' and land speculators had borrowed to the hilt against rising wool and house prices and debt had grown from £39 to £159 per head of population. The economy was based on a vast bubble of speculation that was about to burst. Hughes was one of many new arrivals who helped flood the labour market.[7]

Failing to find employment as a teacher in Brisbane, Hughes spent two knockabout years as an itinerant odd-job man, 'humping his Bluey' (his swag or blanket with his worldly goods rolled inside) mostly on foot in the outback in drought-stricken Queensland and New South Wales. He worked successively as a drover, blacksmith's striker, railway fettler, kitchen hand, cook, labourer, and part-time soldier.

During this period he caught a chill sleeping outside in a frost which made him deaf in one ear (and, incidentally, would give him a useful political prop for the future). His clothes became increasingly ragged and he was sometimes close to starving. He also spent six months as a deck-hand on coastal steamers, and it was in this capacity that he worked his passage to Sydney in 1886. Tempered in the hard crucible of rural unskilled labour, he had picked up his fellows' hard-edged racism – at the time Queensland sugar-cane cutters had to compete with Kanaka labour imported from Melanesia – and delighted in their physical robustness. He also learned to curse. As one of his biographers puts it, '[w]ith buggers, bloodies, bastards and blithering blazes' he became an Australian.[8]

After a series of short-lived jobs, and bouts of unemployment – at one stage he spent a few days living in the harbourside caves near the Domain – he finally found steady work as an oven-maker's mate forging and fitting hinges. With a modest and reliable income, he found lodgings in 'Oleander Lodge', a boarding house near Moore Park, and formed a common law relationship with his landlady's daughter, Elizabeth Cutts, who had a young son from a previous relationship. Over the next several years Billy and Elizabeth had three daughters and two surviving sons (another died as an infant).

The family finally settled in the working-class, dock-side suburb of Balmain where the Hugheses rented a small, weatherboard shop. He worked as a second-hand bookseller, locksmith and door-to-door umbrella mender, and she took in laundry. There, amid the hurly-burly of the docks, Billy read widely, met like-minded young Socialists, and trained himself as a speaker, first as a disciple of the American radical Henry George in the Single Tax League, later in the Socialist League, and then in the Labor Electoral League, a predecessor of the Australian Labor Party. He published his first writing (a letter on the unselfishness of Socialism) in the short-lived Single Tax propaganda newspaper *Democrat*, and won a prize at the Sydney Eisteddfod (for an impromptu speech on 'Myself'). This happened to be in Sydney, but a similar evolution might have occurred in Glasgow, Auckland or Johannesburg.

The time was ripe for radical political action. Shearing strikes in Queensland in 1889 had by 1890–91 escalated into a general maritime strike down the east coast of Australia and miners and waterside workers had also joined in. After a bitter struggle, the men were defeated. Socially and economically, Australia was in a dire crisis. Loans on the London market were unobtainable and the prices of Australian products plummeted. By 1893 most of the banks had crashed, skilled unemployment stood at 30 per cent, unskilled much more and the economy had shrunk by a third.

Hughes, as a self-employed man, had not been directly involved in the strikes, but he was among those 'intellectuals' whose street-corner oratory and pamphleteering advocated a new political approach whereby the trade unions would elect their own representatives to Parliament and achieve by political means what they had failed to do by direct strike action. Hughes and his friend and rival within the Labor Electoral League W A Holman, another recently arrived Londoner with a keen intelligence and the gift of the gab, were at the forefront of this new wave of thought. They read Edward Bellamy, Henry George, Samuel Butler, Herbert Spencer and Karl Marx. However, for Hughes and his associates, society and the state would be restructured not by revolution but by peaceful evolution brought about by Parliamentary action.

Political Labor had burst on the scene in 1891, in the form

Craft unions had been significant in Australian cities since the 1850s and the mass of lesser-skilled workers – shearers, miners, transport workers – had begun to organise in the 1880s. The first Inter-Colonial Trades Union Congress met in Sydney in 1879. Unions endorsed a handful of MPs in this period, but first organised their own party and won significant numbers of seats in the mainland eastern colonies after the failure of the Great Strike of 1890. As a contemporary poem put it:

> Then keep your heads, I say, my boys; your comrades in the town
> Will help you yet to win the vote and put your tyrants down.
> Throw your guns aside, my boys, the ballot is the thing
> They did not have to reckon with when George the Fourth was king.

of the Labor Electoral League, which won 36 seats in the New South Wales Legislative Assembly, enough to bargain for concessions from the Liberal government, and they now aspired for more in the general elections of 1894. As part of Labor's push to expand in the rural areas, in September 1893 Hughes was awarded an eight-month commission – he was to be paid by results – from the powerful Amalgamated Shearers' Union, soon to be renamed the Australian Workers Union (AWU) and the Young Trades Council. Using his public speaking and organising abilities, his task was to travel a sector of outback New South Wales, by bicycle, horse and foot, in the manner of an itinerant Methodist preacher, signing up members for the union and the Labor Electoral League prior to the 1894 New South Wales general election. This marked the real beginning of his political career.

On Hughes's return to Sydney, he and Holman were prime movers in introducing the 'pledge' to the Labor constitution whereby all Labor MPs undertook to maintain solidarity and to vote in Parliament along party lines. His prominence at the 1894 party conference led to his being selected to run for the seat of Lang, centred on Darling Harbour, one of Sydney's inner-city docks. The young Welsh teacher who had arrived as a 'new chum' in 1884 was now fully Australianised; he was in all senses a New South Welshman.

On the Saturday night before the 1894 election Hughes organised a mass demonstration in support of his party. A noisy, half-mile-long procession of workers carrying banners, some men riding on decorated floats, marched to the accompaniment of four bands the mile or so from the Queen's Statue in St James's Square to Prince Alfred Park in Surry Hills where at midnight they heard a succession of rousing speeches. The main banner said, 'Workers, arise, awake! Or ever be fallen' and 100,000 leaflets were distributed.[9] In the poll, Hughes won Lang with a majority of only 105, but his supporters were so jubilant they ran him around the streets in a dog cart and bought him a new suit to improve his appearance when he went to the House. He would remain a colonial or federal MP for the rest of his long life, another 58 years. (In Britain, Lloyd George's career was uncannily similar.) Hughes was now one of 15 'pledged' Labor MPs who, along with 12 'unpledged' Laborites, supported Sir George Reid's 'Free Trade' Liberal government. Five of the 'pledged', including Hughes, were avowed Socialists. But William Morris Hughes, Member of the Legislative Assembly, was now also perforce a gentleman with a salary of £300 a year, a free gold pass on the railways and membership of the colony's most exclusive club.

Hughes entered a legislature in which the Labor members were a small, third force alongside the two big parties, the Free Traders and Protectionists, but potentially Labor might have held the balance of power. Labor's task was to have its programme implemented by means of persuading the party in government to do so. Labor wanted, among other things, an eight-hour day, early (6 p.m.) closing of shops and businesses, old age pensions (in Hughes's words: 'to raise men from the fear of receiving cold crusts and grudging charity'[10]), reform of the Sydney City Council to introduce one-man-one-vote, abolition of the Upper House or Legislative Council ('that tinselled abortion of a House of Lords'[11]) and a new Navigation Act to protect seamen's working conditions.

Hughes, who quickly gained a reputation as a leading spokesman for Labor and was a free trader by conviction, after years of frustration, switched sides dramatically in 1899 with his Labor colleagues to support William Lyne's Protectionists. The final trigger was an outbreak of bubonic plague in the Darling Harbour slums. After inspecting one of the worst streets – there were terraces with ten people to a room and only two filthy open privies jutting out over the harbour to serve their needs – Hughes confronted Lyne in his office and frog-marched him off to inspect the site. They found hordes of bloated, blotchy rats swarming over the slimy harbour wall and dock piles.[12] The plague would take 103 lives in Sydney in 1900. Lyne saw his chance, gained Labor support, cleared the slum and, by giving tenants the vote, reformed the City Council, which had allowed the appalling conditions to persist and a few of whose Aldermen owned some of the hovels in question. Other reforms on the Labor platform followed, and Hughes was lauded by his party.

Also in 1899, Hughes was approached by the languishing Wharf Labourers' Union to be their secretary. He accepted the offer with alacrity as this gave him the chance of an industrial base and a higher public profile. In due course he reorganised the 'wharfies', succeeding through his organisational skills in enlisting two-thirds of all of Sydney's waterfront workers within two years. They were now in a position to compete in the new world of compulsory industrial arbitration which was emerging following the disastrous strikes of the early 1890s. He would remain their very successful voluntary secretary until 1916. He also re-organised, as President, the allied Trolley, Draymen and Carters' Union which represented the men who took the goods from wharf to warehouse.

The wharfies met in St Phillip's Church School Hall and drank in Mann's Hotel, both in Hughes's electorate; and it was the publican at Mann's who first put him in touch with the union. No doubt Hughes selected the union as a test case for the (compulsory) Industrial Arbitration Act (1901) he supported with the Lyne government, as it was Hughes who was the union's principal advocate in negotiating their pay award before the arbitration court in 1902. In that year he was also elected President of the new Waterside Workers' Federation, which combined the waterfront unions across the nation.

A journalist's description of Hughes at a union meeting in 1900 gives a vivid impression of how far he had come, and how he had done it: 'He stood at bay, a sallow, emaciated figure ... in a hall crowded with truculent wharf labourers ... The men were inflamed and were strong for a strike. Hughes was for conciliation ... and he stood up single handed to the angry mob. He reasoned and pleaded with them; he ridiculed them; he swore at them and assailed them as a host of misguided idiots. The meeting ended in wild cheers for him, and there was no strike.' [13]

In the New South Wales Parliament he debated the questions of the day. Labor opposed the despatch of a contingent of troops from New South Wales to the Boer War. Hughes, a visceral Imperialist, spoke out with characteristic pungency: *... when the die is cast, when two nations – ourselves and any other – are engaged in a life and death struggle, it is not the part of any citizen of either of those nations to enquire, 'Why* *am I fighting?' but to fight. But when it comes to a pugilist attacking an infant, and asking his little brother to come and hold the infant while he gets at him, it savours too much of political bravado and swashbuckling to be on all-fours with the noble traditions of the British race.*[14]

The overarching issue in the late 1890s was the political federation of the six Australian colonies; and, on this question, Hughes's position was equivocal. He welcomed federation in theory but objected to the equal representation of each colony, regardless of population size, in the proposed Senate, and therefore opposed the draft constitution. He was also wary of the possible impact on New South Wales of Queensland's decision to allow a small number

> '... when the die is cast, when two nations — ourselves and any other — are engaged in a life and death struggle, it is not the part of any citizen of either of those nations to enquire, "Why am I fighting?" but to fight.'
> **BILLY HUGHES, 18 OCTOBER 1899**

of Japanese traders to enter their colony and (distasteful as his attitude will be to modern sensibilities), he played the race card with great effectiveness: *When he [Premier Reid] says that inside the federal area we shall have a 'white' Australia, what is the good of that when on our northern border [with Queensland] we have a breeding ground for coloured Asiatics, where they will soon be eating the heart's blood out of the white population, where they will multiply and pass over our border in a mighty Niagara, sowing seeds of diseases which will never be eradicated, and which will permanently undermine the constitutional vigour of which the Anglo-Saxon race is so proud ... The Japanese will be supplemented by hordes of Chinese, Kanakas and Javanese.*[15]

Once the constitution was ratified, however, Hughes

announced that he would be a candidate for the new federal or Commonwealth Parliament, to be inaugurated in 1901; and he easily won the seat of West Sydney. Billy Hughes had now arrived on the stage where he was to make his main contribution to Australian life.

2
Nation-building and Troubleshooting, 1901–14

The new federal seat of West Sydney included Hughes's old colonial seat encompassing the Darling Harbour dock area and fanned out into Sydney's working class inner western suburbs. Hughes had no trouble winning it, with almost three-quarters of the votes cast in his favour; and he would keep the seat until 1916. Once in the national Parliament, Hughes and his Labor Party colleagues, from their position as the third strongest party, set about gingering up the Liberal Protectionist governments of Edmund Barton and Alfred Deakin as they went about the task of building and shaping the federal institutions needed for the new nation that would be a 'better Britain' under the southern sun.

Hughes' role was particularly significant in the fields of industrial arbitration, shipping, defence and attempts to extend federal powers. He, with Deakin, would become a central figure in the forging of what later became known as the 'Australian Settlement': a set of inter-locking legislative arrangements which regulated immigration (the White Australia policy), built up domestic industries behind a tariff wall (so-called 'New Protection') and controlled labour conditions by means of compulsory industrial arbitration.[1]

One of the first acts passed by the new Parliament was the Immigration Restriction Act (1901) which sought to control non-European migration by means of administering a 50-word dictation test in a European language other than English. In one celebrated case in the 1930s the language used, which almost guaranteed exclusion, was Gaelic. Hughes approved the legislation and his logic was interesting. In the cloistered seclusion of Parliament and away from the electoral hustings, Hughes argued that *as alien competition aims a blow at the very basis of our industrial system we oppose it*, and *not on account of their colour or religion, because that would be absurd.* He went on to say, however, somewhat contradictorily, that he feared the Japanese with their technical skills, strong work ethic and sheer numbers might swamp the white outpost that was Australia and impose their alien culture and way of life. He thought British Australia needed the White Australia legislation to protect its very existence.[2]

It was a short step from immigration to defence. Barton's government planned to rely on a small professional army backed by a voluntary *levée en masse* of citizens for safeguarding Australia's home soil and the British Fleet, hired at a modest £200,000 per annum, for external protection. Hughes was severely critical of both. He believed that it was every male citizen's compulsory duty to defend his country and the creation of a citizen's militia along Swiss lines was the only answer. Furthermore, Australia should have its own navy under its own command, so that it would not sail away leaving the nation vulnerable, even if this would cost more than double Barton's arrangement. *It is the business of Australians to defend Australia, whether it costs much money or little*, he concluded. These ideas did not bear immediate fruit in 1903, but they did before the decade was out.[3]

Hughes had his first taste of ministerial office in 1904 when he became Minister for External Affairs in Chris Watson's minority Labor administration which lasted less than four months. This was at the impossible time Deakin famously described when there were 'three elevens in the field'. The remarkable thing was that, even for such a brief period of office, Labor showed it was capable of routine administration, and Hughes cut his teeth on keeping ten illegal Chinese out of Darwin and managing the aftermath of an affray in what was still British New Guinea.

The Dutch had annexed West New Guinea in 1828. Colonial Queensland had tried unsuccessfully to annex eastern New Guinea in 1883, only to be rebuffed by the British government. The British finally succumbed in 1884, annexing the south-eastern section, soon after Germany took the north-eastern. British New Guinea was re-named Papua in 1905 and handed over to Australian administration in 1906.

The fragile Labor administration fell, to be succeeded by Liberal administrations under Reid and then Deakin. Deakin described Hughes, on Hughes's leaving office, as like 'the ill-bred urchin whom one sees dragged from a tart-shop kicking and screaming as he goes'.[4] The ministerial tart-shop had not seen the last of little Billy.

During the short-lived Watson regime, Hughes was appointed chairman of a Royal Commission into Navigation. The inquiry, which delved into conditions in all Australia's ports and coastal shipping, ran on well into the next administration and took up much of Hughes's time for over a year, taking him to all parts of the Australian coast. Just as he had organised the waterfront, Hughes now set about regulating the affairs of seamen, eventually bringing them under similar conditions to those which prevailed on land. This, Hughes explained, was not only a matter of industrial welfare but of national defence. Trained merchant seamen would be a good recruiting ground for sailors for the Royal Navy, and in due course an Australian navy.[5]

Deakin, recognising Hughes's maritime expertise and no doubt happy to get him out of his hair for a few months, appointed him

> '[Hughes is] the ill-bred urchin whom one sees dragged from a tart-shop kicking and screaming as he goes.'
>
> **ALFRED DEAKIN, 12 AUGUST 1904**

as part of the Australian delegation to London in March and April 1907 to consult the British Liberal government and the New Zealanders on a common shipping policy. David Lloyd George, the rising star of British politics, chaired proceedings as President of the Board of Trade. He quickly established a lasting rapport with his fellow Welshman, saying of Hughes that he put his case 'with all the tenacity of the ancient race to which you and I belong, and which has enabled us to survive 2,000 years of persecution'. Hughes, writing in the Australian press, praised Lloyd George as a future Prime Minister. Of others he met his opinions were more mixed. Herbert Asquith, another future Prime Minister, had a *cold temperament* and lacked *the magnetism of a party leader*, and the *brilliant* Winston Churchill, his *ambition ... not destined to be satisfied* had *many admirers, but few friends, and his enemies are legion.*[6]

While in Britain, Hughes made a fleeting trip to Wales to see his grandmother, but the highlight of his visit was an invitation by the National Service League to address a mass meeting in Caxton Hall in London chaired by another famous Welshman, Lord Roberts of Kandahar. Here he also met for the first time fellow Liberal Imperialists, Leo Amery and Richard Jebb. These men were the instigators of the National Service

League, which advocated 'national service' in Britain, thus mobilising the loyal working class to the Imperial cause, and was the twin organisation to the Australian National Defence League, the New South Wales branch of which Hughes had become founding secretary in September 1905.

Hughes's Caxton Hall speech shows the stage his thinking had reached at this time. *Conscription*, he said, *produces militarism, universal training destroys it. Conscription produces a caste; universal training deals with the national and places all men on one level.* All civilisation is based on compulsion through the rule of law. *For the Socialist to complain about compulsion is like the devil complaining about sin.* While a voluntary force and the Royal Navy were suitable for overseas service, home defence was a universal duty.[7] Returning to Australia via Canada and the United States he was dismayed to see Italian labourers being used as strike-breakers in New York and interested to read of California's new legislation banning unskilled Japanese workers.

In February 1907, just prior to his departure for England, Hughes had once more demonstrated his negotiating finesse by settling a waterfront strike in New South Wales by means of a direct deal with the ship owners. He returned home to settle, again by direct talks, a three months' old coal-lumpers' dispute; and in 1908 his brinkmanship achieved a fully unionised workforce on the wharves nationwide. His strike-settling abilities had now become legendary. But they were soon to be put to a more severe test.

Syndicalism, in the shape of the 'Wobblies', the American-inspired Industrial Workers of the World (IWW) who called for 'One Big Union' and 'direct action' via general strikes and industrial sabotage, had arrived in Australia by 1908. These ideas, propagated by such passionate advocates as union activists Tom Mann and Harry Holland, spread quickly among the miners and wharfies. The first sign was a failed strike at Broken Hill early in 1909, which saw Holland gaoled for suggesting the men put 'a little ... dynamite' into the struggle after Hughes had opposed the action.[8] Then, in November, Peter Bowling, a radical unionist with IWW connections, led the Newcastle coal miners out on strike against the Vend (the northern coal owners' cartel) and called for the Sydney wharf labourers to boycott Vend coal arriving in coasters. With great difficulty, Hughes talked his wharfies out of striking and very bravely travelled to Newcastle to beard Bowling at a mass meeting of 4,000 miners. This time Hughes was shouted down and the men continued to strike. Cartoonists depicted a miniscule Billy trying to cling onto the horns of a raging bull Bowling.[9] The wharfies, in their turn, also rejected him and he never again regained full control of his old power base. Bowling was arrested and eventually the strike petered out in March 1910 when the men returned to work on the old terms. Though arbitration had manifestly failed, Hughes was lauded for 'saving the State' and putting national above sectional interests, and he briefly became the darling of the capitalist press.[10] It was a sign of things to come.

The face of trade unionism was changing fundamentally as unskilled labour flexed its muscles in the big, 'industrial' unions, where paralysing strikes were the order of the day. These unions were gaining the ascendancy over the old localised, skilled 'craft' based unions. A clever and experienced operator like Hughes could finesse the situation only so many times.

A worsening international situation also had to be confronted. The crushing Japanese naval victory over the Russians in the Battle of Tsushima in the Sea of Japan in May

1905 signalled to Australians and the rest of the world that Japan had arrived as a major power.[11] For Australian politicians with a geostrategic sense, such as Deakin, Hughes and Andrew Fisher, now federal Labor leader, it was clear that, though nominally an ally by virtue of the Anglo-Japanese Treaty of 1902, Japan was now also the greatest threat to Australia's national security.[12] Tsushima provoked the acceleration of Australian defence preparation. In September 1906 Deakin decided to follow Hughes's advice of three years earlier and initiate plans for a modern, free-standing Australian navy. By 1907 he had followed Hughes a step further, advocating compulsory military training for all male citizens. Hughes, for his part, had this accepted as Labor policy at the 1908 party conference. The vagaries of politics delayed action for another two years before Deakin appointed British Field Marshal Lord Kitchener to report on Australia's defence needs, which he duly did in 1910, recommending a home defence force of 80,000 men raised by compulsion.

In the initial debate on Deakin's defence plans Hughes was at his cold-eyed, warm-blooded, forensic and rhetorical best. Even if they were in Australian waters, and this was not guaranteed, the mostly antiquated vessels of the British Pacific squadron were only fit for the 'scrap-heap'. A proper Australian navy was imperative. Furthermore, he argued: *By what virtue are we here today, except by brute force? We came here and displaced those who were placed in possession, if any were, by hand of Providence ... And we talk about peace! We have arrogantly declared that this is to be a white man's country. There are 4,200,000 of us, of whom 21,000 bear arms ... We debar the coloured nations from entry. To the 400,000,000 Chinese, to the 40,000,000 Japanese, flushed with their triumph over a country that humbled every other*

country in Europe in its turn, we have said, 'You must not
come in.' And the weapon with which we propose to keep
them out is an act of Parliament ... Beyond that ... we have
no means of making good our boast. If the White Australia
policy is to be a permanence in this country, there must be
behind it a sufficient force of White Australians ready ... to
make good their claim.[13]

The Deakin initiative led in due course to the inauguration
by Hughes in 1910, under the Fisher Labor government in
which Hughes was Attorney General, of compulsory military
training for youths aged 11 to 17 years and adults of 18 to 26
years. It was a veritable manpower revolution and between
1911 and 1915 some 636,000 were trained.[14] This compulsory
military training scheme was a significant departure from
British practice and unique in the British world.

Deakin had failed, however, to legislate for a navy. The
first Fisher government had in 1908 endorsed Australia's
naval director Captain W R Creswell's plans for a coastal
protection, 'brown-water' navy of 23 destroyers and a patrol
boat; but these had not been implemented. Deakin's 1909–10
administration invited the 16 battleships of the American
'Great White Fleet' to visit Australia later that year, and advocated an ocean-going, 'blue-water' navy, based upon cruisers
and submarines. This plan was enacted by Hughes in 1910
during the second Fisher government. The upshot was that
the battlecruiser *Australia*, three light cruisers, six destroyers and three submarines were laid down, designed strategically to act alone or as part of a larger British Pacific Fleet.
They sailed into Sydney Heads on 4 October 1913, on which
day Australia became the first British Dominion to establish
its own navy.[15] When these plans were well in train Hughes
announced to Parliament with some considerable satisfaction,

and a little exaggeration, that *we have placed a fleet on the water, and an army on the land, the like of which has not been seen in our time.*[16] Should Japan now turn hostile, and Hughes and Fisher were not at all reassured by the renewal of the Anglo-Japanese Treaty in 1911, it would now need to send more than a raiding party to Australian shores.

Watson had stepped down as Labor leader in October 1907 and the party had chosen Fisher, a Scottish-born coal miner the same age as Hughes who had migrated to Queensland at the same time. He was dour and reliable. The party had chosen, as the parliamentary historian put it, 'Scottish caution over Welsh panache'; but Hughes remained, in the *Sydney Morning Herald*'s term, the 'fiery particle' who animated the party and the electorate.[17] The first Fisher government lasted some six months, governing only with the consent of the Deakinites, and achieved little other than deciding that Canberra would be the national capital and the location of the federal Parliament. On 27 May 1909 the Deakinites switched sides, ousting Labor and paving the way for Deakin's 'Fusion' government which united 'free trade' and 'protectionist' MPs. When Deakin was called 'Judas', Hughes quipped that it *is not fair – to Judas [who] ... did not gag the man whom he betrayed, nor did he fail to hang himself afterwards.*[18]

Be this as it may, Labor still supported Deakin's progressive legislation. Earlier it had helped introduce invalid and old age pensions (1908); now it helped pass acts for compulsory military training, the navy and a permanent formula for transferring federal revenues to the states beyond 1910 when

> 'We have placed a fleet on the water, and an army on the land, the like of which has not been seen in our time.'
>
> **BILLY HUGHES, 26 JUNE 1912**

the 'Braddon' clause expired. This clause, Section 87 in the Constitution, gave three-quarters of the customs revenues to the states for the first ten years of the federation. The new formula gave the states 25 shillings per capita each year from federal receipts.

The elections of February 1910, however, brought Labor to power for the first time in its own right with Fisher as Prime Minister and Hughes once more Attorney General. Hughes, in the words of the Labor Premier of New South Wales, was 'the leading mind in the new government' and Fisher the 'conscientious and manageable puppet'.[19] What is more, Hughes got his head when he served as Acting Prime Minister for two long periods: October to December 1910, when Fisher was in South Africa, and April to August 1911, when the Prime Minister attended an Imperial Conference in London.

The Fisher government, with control of both houses of Parliament, was able to introduce a number of important nation-building measures, in all of which Hughes was seminally involved. The Northern Territory was transferred from South Australian to federal administration, a graduated land tax created a reliable federal income stream, a Commonwealth Bank was founded and Australian postage stamps – the penny kangaroo – and currency were introduced. Doubters, soon proved wrong, nick-named the first paper notes 'Fisher's flimsies'. (Before its devaluation in 1929 the Australian pound equated to the pound sterling.) In addition, as has been noted, a properly articulated scheme for compulsory military training was instituted and a structure for the new navy put in place. There were also plans for an east-west trans-continental railway and a government shipping line.

Labor was lucky to be elected just as an economic boom was gathering momentum. After the disastrous 1890s and the sluggish early years of the century, trade had begun to pick up and with it immigration. Some 400,000 new migrants arrived in the three years of Labor rule, the highest rate since the early 1880s. The motor car began to make its mark on Australian roads. As a sign of its modernity, the new government purchased for £850 its own car, a four-cylinder Renault with a myrtle green torpedo body and red trim, capable of 50 mph. The first aeroplane flight with passengers was made in 1911.

A major problem for the federal government, however, was its lack of control over the levers of the economy. The High Court had ruled that arbitration was essentially a state matter, and there were no powers for the regulation of price-fixing trusts and cartels. The land tax was a partial solution, as were the renegotiation of the Braddon clause and the establishment of an Inter-State Commission, provided for in the constitution as a standing tribunal policing its commerce clauses. But the key, as Hughes saw it, was a referendum to change the constitution and give the federal government more powers.

Hughes' ambitious referendum put four proposals to the electors on 26 April 1911: replacement of arbitration by sweeping powers to the federal government over wages and work conditions, power in inter-state industrial disputes, power to control monopolies, and the right of the federal government to establish its own businesses in areas where a monopoly was deemed to exist. Yet, despite his most energetic efforts at persuasion, the proposals were decisively defeated in every state except Western Australia. This was not least because the state governments, including most prominently the Labor administration in New South Wales led by Hughes' friend Holman, were opposed to the dilution of their own powers.

Failing to control the monopolistic practices of the coal

Vend and the Colonial Sugar Refining Company through the High Court, Hughes girded his loins for a second tilt at a referendum and for stacking the High Court by appointing sympathetic judges. In 1912 he tried to shoehorn his Commonwealth Crown Solicitor, Charles Powers, and A B Piddington, a rising Sydney barrister not yet a King's Counsel, onto the High Court Bench. The *Bulletin* described putting the two forward as 'not so much mistakes as grim tragedies'.[20] There was uproar in the legal profession over this blatant placemanship and Piddington withdrew his candidature, leaving Hughes' scheme in tatters. There remained the second referendum attempt in May 1913; but it, too, failed, though by a narrower margin. The national election, held at the same time, saw Labor lose to Joseph Cook's Liberals.

In private life Hughes had also had a rackety but upwardly mobile journey. His incessant peregrinations by rail from Sydney to Melbourne to attend Parliament in the temporary federal capital[21] had put his marriage under great strain, as his *de facto* wife remained in Sydney in their comfortable house at Gore Hill on the lower North Shore of the harbour. Lizzie, after a long period of neglect and invalidism, died of heart failure, aged 42, on 1 September 1906. Hughes, who was not present, received a poignantly understated letter written a fortnight before she died. 'Good night, Will: always remember this: that once I loved you very dearly and tho we may drift apart in the future: I shall always remain, your faithful wife, E. Hughes.'[22]

Thereafter Hughes' elder daughter Ethel kept house for him and the children in rented accommodation in Melbourne where they were placed in good private schools, as befitted the children of a Cabinet Minister on £1,000 a year. On 26 June 1911, a public holiday, Hughes took a day off from his

Acting Prime Minister activities to marry 'again', at Christ Church, South Yarra, a church favoured by Melbourne high society, though the marriage was a low-key affair. His bride was Mary Campbell, aged 37, a trained nurse and the second daughter of a prosperous flour miller and grazier from southern New South Wales. Their only child, Helen, was born in 1916. With his family life now secure and a growing political reputation, Hughes was set for an assault on the Prime Ministership should an opportunity present itself.

Such was the potential for progression in this relatively seamless British world that an adult from a relatively humble background but with talent could emigrate from Britain and within ten years become a colonial MP, in another ten a Federal Minister, and less than a decade later a contender for the Prime Ministership of the new nation. In those days, Britishness, albeit with an Australian twist, was an asset not a liability. Hughes's nation-building and trouble-shooting would continue, but now it would be in the demanding crucible of a war to preserve the nation and Empire.

3
War, 1914–16

The British declaration of war on 4 August 1914 found Australia in the throes of a federal election campaign, during which Andrew Fisher would clinch victory for Labor by capturing the patriotic mood of '"mafficking" madness'[1] and pronouncing that 'Australians would stand by our own [by which he meant Britain] to help and defend her to our last man and our last shilling'.[2] The Cook government had already promised to raise 20,000 volunteers for the Australian Imperial Force (AIF) by Christmas; and, in the event, 50,000 were enlisted. But it was the Fisher government which despatched them; and in that government the Deputy Leader and Attorney-General was William Morris Hughes.

Hughes, who saw the War from the outset as a life-or-death struggle between nations as much as armies, lost no time in passing the War Precautions Act and the Trading with the Enemy Act. These wide-sweeping acts, more draconian than their British equivalents, allowed, among other things, the suspension of freedom of speech, of trade, and of the right to trial. It is said that Thomas Bavin, a New South Wales politician, once asked Solicitor-General Robert Garran, 'Would it be an offence under the War Precautions Regulations …?' and Garran replied 'Yes' before he could finish.[3] Later in the War Hughes would say, with only a little exaggeration, that his use of the War Precautions Act's more than 100 regulations enabled him to personally *govern Australia with a fountain pen … a blank sheet of paper* and the assistance of Garran.[4]

One of Hughes's first targets was the German base metals trade with Australia. Zinc, lead and copper were essential for the production of munitions and were third in importance among Australian exports after wool and wheat. Before the War started, all the zinc had been supplied on long-term contracts through two German firms which controlled the overseas refineries: Mertons of London and the Australian Metal Company of Melbourne, which in turn were owned by Frankfurt Metallgesellschaft. Sixty per cent of the lead and copper was locally refined but the rest went through two other German firms: Aaron Hirsh for lead and Beer Sondheimer for copper.[5]

Hughes consulted the Australian producers and eventually hired a retired Melbourne metallurgist, John Higgins, who had been put out of business by the Germans, to establish the Australian Metals Exchange in September 1915 which co-ordinated the sale of some £35 million worth of metals by the War's end. Hughes also collaborated with W L Baillieu and W S Robinson of the Collins House group of companies to build new zinc and copper refineries in Australia, thus keeping value-added production in Australian and British hands. Robinson was the 39-year-old son of the economics editor of Melbourne's most influential newspaper, *The Age*, renowned for its advocacy of high protection. He was a partner in a number of mining and smelting companies, and was to become a key adviser to Hughes as the War progressed.[6]

Wool was next. After difficulties with German proxies buying large amounts of the Australian clip, in the Australian auctions and in those in neutral countries, particularly the United States, the government agreed in October 1915 to suspend all sales of wool to countries other than Britain. The Australian woolgrowers argued that the embargo had more to do with starving American woollens manufacturers who competed with the traditional Bradford market for supplies. Through Hughes' doughty advocacy, the woolgrowers eventually persuaded the British government in November 1916 to purchase the whole Australian clip for the duration of the War at a price 55 per cent higher than the pre-war price. This guaranteed price was mutually beneficial: it cushioned the Australian growers and also proved a good deal for the British since the open market price went even higher. Furthermore, given the shipping shortage, much of the wool was stockpiled and destined not to get to Britain until the peace. Hughes always claimed, quite correctly, that his hard bargaining gained the growers an extra halfpenny of the 15½ pence per pound agreed. Higgins, who set up the Metals Exchange, was appointed to chair the Central Wool Committee to oversee the sales.[7]

Wheat proved more difficult to sell than wool and metals. Australia lacked a key position in the international grain market, with competition from the United States, Canada, India, Argentina, Romania and Russia, all of which suppliers were closer to the European consumers. In addition, wheat took up much more shipping space relative to its value than did wool or metals, and the latter were preferred as cargo. Nevertheless, after drought and poor harvests between 1911 and 1914, an opportunity to sell the bumper 1915 wheat crop came in 1916 when there was a partial breakdown in the North

American and Argentine supply, which had been much cheaper to obtain under war conditions.[8] At the end of 1915, Hughes, working principally with Frederick Hagelthorn, Victoria's Agriculture Minister, set up a Wheat Board to pool wheat sales and a year later sold 112 million bushels (of a crop of 179 million) to the British government at the favourable price of 4s 9d free-on-board. Hughes also negotiated with the British government a loan of £11 million to cover most of the £15 million cost of advance purchase. The farmers were soon to be very grateful that the wheat was bought not only at a good price but before rather than after it was shipped.[9] Following on under the same agreement, a further 116 million bushels were sold on the same terms from the 1917 crop. At the time, this combined sale was claimed to be the largest ever concluded.[10]

Dairy products, sugar, leather, tallow and a number of other commodities were also pooled under a variety of federal-state-private enterprise tie-up deals and sold to Britain for the duration of the War. Meat exports were essentially a Queensland issue and, once an act of that state's Parliament gave Britain exclusive rights, some £300 million worth were sold to, or through, Britain during the War, mostly for the British Army. The British Board of Trade also guaranteed the shipping of it.[11] Depending on one's perspective, these measures could be seen either by the left as 'war socialism' or by the right as protection of vital industries at a difficult time in the international markets. Doubtless, Hughes was happy for both sides to think as they did.

War finance is a thorny subject but the overall shape of the Australian position is readily put in summary. It was hoped that the cost of the War would be met from domestic sources, revenue and loans, but this proved far too optimistic. Unemployment and national development necessitated a continuation of both federal and state loans raised from Britain, not least to build the transcontinental railway, finished in 1917. There was some adverse comment in British Treasury circles that Australia was borrowing money to employ men domestically who should otherwise have enlisted in the armed services; but this was muted as it was understood that the Australian economy was under stress and needed propping up if the large Australian army was to stay in the field in France, Belgium and Palestine.[12] The cessation of immigration and its massive impact on the building trade, along with the shipping shortage, meant that Australia's GDP actually shrank by a tenth during the War.

In the face of this crisis, a Premiers' Conference met in July 1915, and all states except the largest, New South Wales, agreed with the federal government to approach the London market together in future. By War's end the states combined had raised and spent £99.7 million, mostly on development projects, and the federal government had spent at least £13 million on public works. The War itself cost the federal government (by 1919) £376.99 million, £250 million of which had been raised by local subscription. Once war pensions and gratuities are taken into account this ballooned to £831.28 million by 1934.[13] On top of this, some £14 million was raised by voluntary patriotic funds.[14] Paying off the debt would take decades.

The most immediate and significant contribution from Australia, however, came in the form of military manpower. Whereas compulsory military training for home defence was mandatory for juvenile and adult males, enlistment for the AIF was, and would remain, voluntary. The AIF fought initially against the Turks at Gallipoli and in defence of the Suez Canal in 1915, and from 1916 mostly on the Western Front.

QUARTERLY ENLISTMENTS IN THE AIF, 1914–16		
1914	August–December	52,565
1915	January–April	33,758
1915	May–August	85,320
1915	September–December	46,834
1916	January–April	66,082
1916	May–August	29,756
1916	September–December	25,512

Source: Calculated from Scott, *Australia During the War*, Appendix 3.

The table shows the dimensions and pattern of voluntary recruitment for 1914–16 by the quarter.

As can be readily seen, numbers peaked in the middle of 1915 (after the AIF received their 'baptism of fire' in the Gallipoli landing on 25 April). They picked up again in early 1916 (when the bulk of the AIF moved to France). But numbers tailed off thereafter. It was estimated that it would take some 9,500 recruits per month to keep the AIF's five divisions in the field. By the middle of 1916, this figure was not being met and the prospect of replenishment for the major battles which were inevitable in the spring and summer of 1917 was increasingly grim.

As a result of the War Census Act, hurried through Parliament by Hughes in July 1915, in a December 'Call to Arms', all males between 18 and 44 years of age were asked two critical, leading questions: If willing to enlist now? Reply 'Yes' or 'No'. If you reply 'Yes' you will be given a fortnight's notice before being called up. If not willing to enlist now, are you willing to enlist at a later date? Reply 'Yes' or 'No', and if willing, state when. If not willing to enlist, state the reason why, as explicitly as possible. Signature in full. Write your names distinctly.[15]

Consequently, the Commonwealth Statistician G H Knibbs

estimated there were some 600,000 fit, eligible men.[16] Addressing the question of whether the census anticipated conscription, in July 1915 Hughes stated: *I do not believe conscription is necessary*, though *I do not say that the future may not hold within it possibilities which may shatter our present conceptions of what is necessary, for no man can say what this frightful war may yet involve.*[17] Four months later, Hughes was Prime Minister; and a year later, he would be confronted with just the situation he had anticipated.

Throughout 1915 Fisher had increasingly delegated the deal-making at the heart of government to Hughes, himself preferring to preside rather than lead. While this strategy had the virtue of keeping Fisher above the political fray, it gave Hughes an increasing appetite for power. It also meant that Hughes became the prime target for the vocal handful of socialist-minded idealists of the Victorian Left, led by Frank Anstey, who opposed the War and the restrictions on civil liberties inherent in the War Precautions Act and other Hughesian measures.

> 'I do not believe conscription is necessary ... [though] I do not say that the future may not hold within it possibilities which may shatter our present conceptions of what is necessary, for no man can say what this frightful war may yet involve.'
>
> **BILLY HUGHES, 14 JULY 1915**

Hughes was also opposed by the 'industrials' – those increasingly influential leaders of strong trade unions who saw the Labor government as their direct instrument and who otherwise would not flinch at direct industrial action to achieve their goals. They felt particularly betrayed by the government's inability to control prices and trusts following the failure of the 1911 and 1913 referenda. Hughes tried to assuage them by passing acts for a new referendum on these issues and setting of the poll for 11 December 1915.

Before this, however, on 28 October Hughes at last became Prime Minister when Fisher, weary of the strains of office, resigned to become High Commissioner in London.[18] As was his wont, Hughes immediately made two important decisions. He would abandon the referendum and he would travel almost straightaway to Britain. The latter was in response to an invitation to all Dominion Prime Ministers to visit, and was prompted by a need to get a feel for how the AIF might be used in France, whence they were about to proceed after withdrawing from Gallipoli; to press Australia's case over Japan for annexation of the German Pacific colonies; and to clinch a number of major commodity export deals.

The referendum decision was prompted by a Premiers Conference at which Hughes discovered that none of the state leaders was enthusiastic for the transfer of powers a successful referendum would have entailed; and the Labor Premiers of New South Wales and Queensland, W A Holman and T J Ryan, suggested that concerted state legislation transferring the powers only for the War's duration was a tidier way to proceed. In the event, Hughes took them at their word and set the referendum aside, only to find later that the states did not honour their side of the bargain. Hughes was left carrying the baby and the Socialists and Industrials in the federal Labor Party never forgave him for this 'betrayal'.[19] Fortuitously, while Hughes was absent in Britain, the High Court's ruling in *Farey v Burvett*, in which it maintained that fixing the bread price was a legitimate exercise of the Defence power, gave the federal government all the wartime powers it needed and the referendum idea lapsed, though the Left still licked their wounds.[20]

Sir Ronald Munro Ferguson, the Scottish laird and

politician who was Australia's wartime Governor-General, wrote some perceptive pen portraits of the man who had become his new Prime Minister: 'He has not been regarded as a very reliable politician, and has made many enemies. He is very small and nervous, very Welsh, able, active and determined.' And three years further on with more ambivalence: 'Mr. Hughes gives orders like a Roman centurion and seldom devolves responsibility on anybody. His impatience and autocratic ways destroy initiative in others yet he has the qualities of his defects ...'[21]

Before embarking for London, Hughes stumped the country in a major recruiting drive to raise an extra 50,000 men, over and above the monthly quota of 9,500. In this 'Call to Arms' he stressed that the War could only be won by the total mobilisation of resources. He pointed to the War Census Act and to his pooling of Australian primary products for export. While some saw this as a prelude to conscription, Hughes himself argued that if voluntarism were widely supported compulsion would not be necessary. No sooner had he landed in England, than Hughes made contact with Keith Murdoch, a 30-year-old Melbourne journalist who had been running the cable service to Australia since September. Through Murdoch he came to the notice of Lord Northcliffe, who was proprietor of *The Times*, and other press barons. Northcliffe was running his own national press campaign

> '[Hughes] is not unlike his countryman Lloyd George. His judgement is better; his insight clear; his capacity for affairs great. He is highly strung and at times violent. I have always found him agreeable. Few men are more entertaining ... He stands out above his own party in intellect, courage and skill. He is the right man to be Prime Minister.'
>
> **SIR RONALD MUNRO FERGUSON,**
> **8 NOVEMBER 1915**

advocating total mobilisation and Hughes's speaking skills were quickly enlisted to the cause. Hughes was in the right place at the right time.

The Asquith government was faltering and Hughes' 'live wire' energy[22] contrasted with its relative lethargy. Apart from Hughes, in government only the dynamic Welsh heir apparent Lloyd George, at the time revolutionising production as Minister for Munitions, was pointing the way forward. Outside government, a small collection of one-nation, Empire-minded Conservatives, led by Lord Milner and Leopold Amery, were agitating for change and soon made common cause with Hughes. Tariff reform and scientific, Imperial and industrial organisation would not only win the War but set the Empire fair for the years of peace. Hughes spoke often and well and was lionised or duchessed wherever he went. Among other engagements, he spoke at the first Anzac Day service at Westminster Abbey, visited the Grand Fleet at Rosyth, dined with the King and Queen, was sworn a Privy Councillor, and received a number of honorary degrees and freedoms of cities. Murdoch edited his speeches, read already in the press by millions, and published them as *'The Day' – and After*.

Hughes' graphic, inflamed and widely reported oratory left little to the imagination. Germany was *sweeping over the earth like some stupendous cataract of burning lava [which] … threatened to destroy mankind*. German influence *ran like a cancer, throughout the fair body of British trade and commerce*. He was stamping it out in Australia and Britain should do the same. The war had to be won on all fronts.[23] It struck a deep emotional chord in beleaguered Britain.

Asquith was not sure what to do with Hughes, but he agreed to make him part of the British delegation to an Allied Economic Conference in Paris, where his red-in-tooth-and-claw attitude to economic warfare and making Germany pay won new admirers among the French. The Conference's resolutions against trading with the enemy, however, were far less draconian than those Hughes had recommended based on his Australian legislation.[24]

The Sydney *Bulletin* cartoonist David Low, who was later to have an illustrious career in Britain, epitomised the popular conception of Hughes' impact in Britain by depicting him alone at one end of the British Cabinet room, standing on one leg, beating the table with one arm, the other raised in the air, with papers and chairs flying everywhere, and a worried Asquith and Lloyd George sheltering at the other end of the table. The caption read 'Asquith: David, talk to him in Welsh and pacify him!'[25]

In the deeper private recesses of Whitehall and the City of London, Hughes had another impact. He negotiated the wheat loan and sale, and, with W S Robinson's help, sold Australia's zinc and other base metals. But he struck a snag over shipping. The Shipping Committee of the Board of Trade refused to release sufficient freighters – he wanted 50 – to carry Australia's wheat and wool to market. In wartime the merchant fleet was severely depleted and supplies had to be obtained by the shortest route, usually from the Americas, regardless of higher initial prices there. After several refusals, Hughes came up with a typically robust solution. Behind the backs of the British officials, he arranged to buy 16 steamers and then embarrassed Asquith into agreeing not to requisition them (these vessels became the nucleus of the Australian government-owned Commonwealth Shipping Line). Now at least some of Australia's wheat and wool would find its way to Britain.[26]

Hughes was less successful over the German Pacific islands.

The German islands north of the Equator had been occupied by the Japanese. This was despite their having been ceded to the British Empire (in this case Australia and New Zealand) in November 1914, when the Germans had surrendered to an Australian force at their Pacific capital Rabaul in New Guinea. The British had later agreed in 1915 to the Japanese keeping the islands they occupied (and formalised the matter in a secret treaty of February 1917) and were less than forthcoming about it to Hughes, who was furious when he found out. A compromise was reached: he would stay quiet in public during the War but reserved the right to re-open the question during the peace negotiations.[27]

While Hughes toured the country arguing the case for an increased war effort, the British Parliament was introducing and implementing military conscription under the Military Service Act, passed in February 1916. All single men and childless widowers aged 18 to 41 years of age were liable. New Zealand would follow suit in August.[28] The British move raised the spectre of Australian conscription.

Even before he had left Australia, Hughes had received trade union delegations against conscription; yet, on the other hand, he was aware that a Universal Service League had been founded to argue for it. Given his known personal attitudes to the War and to compulsory military training, Hughes had no choice but to address the issue. Even as planning for a major offensive on the Somme in the summer went ahead, voluntary recruitment figures for the AIF were declining. Hughes headed home to Australia in June into a developing political cyclone.

4

The Battle for Conscription, 1916–18

'William the Great', as the Opposition Leader dubbed him, returned to Australia to a hero's welcome at Fremantle, 'covered with honour and glory'.[1] Before he left London, it appears he had arranged through the Commandant of AIF Headquarters in Britain, Brigadier General R M Anderson (in civilian life an old crony of Hughes' in the New South Wales Public Service) to have the British Army Council cable a request for an additional 20,000 recruits. These were to make up for the dreadful Australian losses at Pozières on the Somme (where there had been 23,000 casualties in six weeks as compared to some 26,000 at Gallipoli in eight months). The cable also requested 16,500 men per month for three months thereafter. Given that only 6,345 enlisted in that month, such inflated numbers could probably only be found by introducing conscription. The cable arrived, it seemed by happy coincidence, on the eve of Hughes' meeting with the 'caucus' of federal Labor MPs to discuss recruitment.[2]

In Hughes's seven-month absence abroad, battle lines had been drawn on the issue. Australia's largest union, the AWU, had voted against conscription, as had the trades halls in Sydney and Melbourne, a special inter-state trades union congress, and the Labor parties in Queensland, New South Wales and Victoria.[3] Pearce had written to Hughes in May that a majority of the federal parliamentary party was 'strongly opposed'; and W G Higgs, the federal Treasurer, wrote in August that the issue would 'split' the party into 'fragments'.[4] On the other side, the chambers of commerce and of manufacturers, the farmers' and settlers' associations, the Liberal Conference, many local government bodies and nearly all of the press were in support. At mass meetings of welcome in Perth, Adelaide, Melbourne and Sydney, Hughes kept his counsel, saying enigmatically, *I shall do my duty fearlessly, and I shall look to the people of Australia to support me.*[5]

'Caucus' is a Native American term from the Algonquin word for adviser, which was in common use in the United States at the time to denote meetings of political parties to select members for office. In Australian political usage, it means a meeting of all elected Labor MPs from both Houses of Parliament.

As his party was against him and it controlled the Senate, Hughes was not in a position, politically, to introduce conscription by Act of Parliament. With Opposition support a bill might pass through the House of Representatives, but he did not have the numbers in the upper house. He might have introduced it by regulation under the War Precautions Act, but his party would have revolted and he might have lost the leadership. Bearing all this in mind, he plumped for a referendum: if he could persuade the electorate, its decision would sway the party. After four days of argument, the caucus voted narrowly, 23 to 21, to have a referendum. Two days later Parliament set the date for 28 October.

Hughes now proceeded to make three tactical errors. First, he called up, under the compulsory military training regulations, all eligible males for a 21-day camp, no doubt thinking he would then be ahead of the game should the referendum pass. Instead, this concentrated the minds of many families who might lose bread-winners under conscription. Second, when, entirely coinci-dentally and unknown to him, a boatload of 98 Maltese men ofs-military age arrived in Australia, he was landed with the sobriquet William 'Maltese' Hughes, for supposedly sending Australian-born men off to fight while introducing cheap, non-British, immigrant labour to replace them. The ship and its unwanted passengers were diverted to Noumea, but the propaganda damage was done. Third, in Sydney, 12 members of the IWW were arraigned before a show trial on charges of plotting to burn Sydney to the ground and found guilty.[6]

The Industrial Workers of the World (IWW) never had more than a couple of hundred members in Australia, but their newspaper *Direct Action* was widely read for its violent, anti-war and anti-capitalist rhetoric. Hughes banned the organization in 1916. The 'Twelve' were released from gaol in 1920 and 1921 when a Royal Commission appointed by a state Labor government found the original evidence under which they had been charged to have been insufficient.

Meanwhile, Hughes sought political advantage from the Irish Question. The bloody suppression of the Easter Rebel-lion was still fresh in the minds of Australia's Irish (some 20 per cent of the population were of Irish heritage). Hughes had tried, unsuccessfully, to have the British government asso-ciate his name with the lifting of martial law in Ireland. The bishops and archbishops of the Catholic Church in Australia, synonymous with the 'Irish' population, were mostly either for conscription or neutral, except for Dr Daniel Mannix, the Coadjutor Archbishop in Melbourne, whose Sinn Fein sym-pathies led him to denounce it as 'a hateful thing'. 'Easter Week stirred the Paddy,' Anstey later wrote.[7]

ARCHBISHOP DANIEL MANNIX

Daniel Mannix, tall, spare and quite as acerbic as Hughes, was born in 1864 in Charleville, Cork, Ireland, making him two years younger than the Prime Minister. He had a distinguished academic career, culminating in the Presidency of Maynooth College, Ireland's principal Catholic seminary, before moving to Melbourne in 1912. Mannix's debating skills and showmanship matched Hughes' own, which infuriated the Prime Minister. Hughes toyed with having Mannix deported but decided against it. In 1920, during the Irish Troubles, Mannix's inflammatory speeches while visiting the United States led to the British government sending a destroyer to stop him landing in Ireland, marooning him at Penzance. He returned to Melbourne and a long career both in the Church and as an *eminence grise* in Labor politics. He died almost a centurion in 1963.

An idea of the levels of bitterness in the campaign can be had from the battle of the pamphlets.[8] Most effective on the Anti side was 'The Blood Vote', a poem accompanied by a picture of a horned, cloven-hoofed devil, a worried woman and a pencil dripping with blood, which read in part:

> Why is your face so white, Mother?
> Why do you choke for breath?
> O, I have dreamt in the night, my son,
> That I doomed a man to death.
>
> ...
>
> They put a dagger into my grasp,
> It seemed but a pencil then,
> I did not know it was a fiend agasp
> For the priceless blood of men.

Another poster had a child imploring his mother to 'Vote No Mum. They'll take Dad next.'

On the pro-conscription side, the 'Anti's Creed' was

perhaps the most virulent. From 1917 and the even more desperate second referendum campaign, it read, in part:

> I believe the men at the Front should be sacrificed.
> I believe we should turn dog on them.
> ...
> I believe in the sanctity of my own life.
> I believe in taking all the benefit and none of the risks.
> I believe it was right to sink the *Lusitania*.
> ...
> I believe in the I.W.W.
> I believe in Sinn Fein.
> ...
> I believe in the massacre of Belgian priests.
> ...
> I believe that Nurse Cavell got her just deserts.
> ...
> I believe in general strikes.
> I believe in burning Australian haystacks.
> ...
> I believe in handing Australia over to Germany.
> I believe I'm worm enough to vote No.[9]

When the vote came the anti-conscriptionists won by the narrowest of margins, some 72,476 votes in an electorate of 2.3 million: Victoria, Western Australia and Tasmania voted 'For'; and New South Wales, Queensland and South Australia 'Against'. The difference was about the size of a large sporting crowd at the Melbourne Cricket Ground. Hughes wrote to Murdoch, *The Ides of March have come and gone and Caesar still lives!*, and to Andrew Bonar Law, the British Colonial Secretary, he claimed he would have won *in spite*

*of the official Labor organisations being against us: in spite
of the Irish vote, in spite of the shirkers, if the farmers and
Conservatives had stood by us.*[10] His secretary Percy Deane
later put it more graphically, blaming the 'offal-stained clod-
hoppers of New South Wales' who feared for their 'supply of
teat-pullers' and voted 'No'.[11]

Conventional wisdom at the time had the Catholics, trade
unionists, Irish, women and farmers voting 'No' and the
Protestants, businessmen, graziers, recent immigrants and
urban middle classes 'Yes'. But this does not add up arith-
metically: for instance, many Protestants, at 80 per cent of
the population, must have voted 'No', and many women and
workers 'Yes'. Careful cliometric analysis suggests, indeed,
that farmer-owners and women tended to vote 'Yes', while
rural labourers voted 'No', along with a large cohort of their
fellow workers in the cities. The soldiers voted 'Yes', though
those actually at the Front voted 'No'.[12]

After the vote Hughes met the Labor caucus and, following
a stormy meeting, led 25 MPs (14 from the House of Representatives and 11 Senators) out of the party to form what
became the National Labor Party. He then, with Opposition
support, formed a new minority government and, after some
months of hard bargaining, made common cause with Joseph
Cook's Liberals and incorporated them into a 'Win the War'
coalition (he gave them six Ministers to National Labor's five).
As Nationalists, this new coalition party fought a general election in May 1917 and won comprehensively. The rump of the
old Labor Party won only 22 of 75 seats in the House of Representatives and none of the 18 Senate seats on offer. Hughes
gained a clear majority in both chambers. Clearly, though a
great many Australians were against conscription, they were
not against continuing to fight the War with volunteers. It is

QUARTERLY ENLISTMENTS IN THE AIF, 1917–18	
1917 January–April	19,134
1917 May–August	15,684
1917 September–December	10,283
1918 January–April	8,561
1918 May–August	13,128
1918 September–November	7,194

Source: Calculated from Scott, *Australia During the War*, Appendix 3.

revealing of the complexity of Australia's wartime society, for instance, that trade unionists were a higher proportion of the AIF than they were of the general population, and that Catholics enlisted at a slightly higher rate per capita than Protestants.[13] In the election, Hughes gave up his now unwinnable West Sydney seat for the more congenial Bendigo in rural Victoria: a unique move in the Australian context, where politicians might change parties, but not states, and also a measure of Hughes's remarkably protean appeal.

The most pressing problem facing the new government remained recruitment. The British authorities were calling for 140,000 new recruits in 1917 just to keep the AIF's five divisions in the field (four on the Western Front and one in Palestine) as well as the raising of a sixth division, which would require 20,000 more men. It was estimated that there were still at least 350,000 more eligibles in Australia.[14] A new recruitment organisation was set up with its own director general and paid officials in every local government area, but the results were disappointing:

Furthermore, events seemed to be conspiring for Australia to re-visit the question of conscription. In April 1917 the United States entered the War and President Woodrow Wilson immediately conscripted 500,000 men. In October, after a bitterly-fought election, Canada also introduced conscription. This meant that, of the English-speaking countries, the United Kingdom (with the exception of Ireland, where the attempt to introduce it met with fierce opposition), the United States, Canada, Newfoundland and New Zealand conscripted, while Australia and South Africa did not.

It is interesting to ponder what an ideal level of enlistment might have been. Evidence collected post-war suggests that, for their economies, Britain and the Dominions ideally ought to have enlisted about 40 per cent of available manpower. Thus, Britain over-conscripted at 53 per cent, as did New Zealand, while Canada under-conscripted at 38 per cent. Australia's voluntary rate was 39 per cent, putting it just under the ideal, but interestingly so was Canada's.[15]

Needless to say, the pressure was mounting on Hughes and Australia to introduce conscription by Act of Parliament. This grew irresistible once Russia had collapsed in the wake of the October Revolution, thereby potentially releasing 48 German divisions for the Western Front and giving the Germans numerical superiority there.[16] This was the war-changing event Hughes had anticipated when he said he could not rule out another referendum, which he duly announced for 20 December.

The year 1917 was a difficult one all round. Unrestricted submarine warfare had badly affected the shipping of supplies to Britain and had brought the United States into the War. Unprecedentedly bloody battles in the spring at Bullecourt (7,000 casualties) and in the autumn at Passchendaele (11,750 casualties) depleted the AIF markedly. Between July and November there were 38,093 casualties in total. At home, switching off two of the great engines of growth – immigration and investment – had caused the economy to shrink and conditions to worsen: the cost of living jumped by over a quarter, real wages fell by over ten per cent, and strikes proliferated. In 1917 there were 4,599,658 man-days lost to strikes, as opposed to 1,090,395 days in 1914, 583,225 in 1915, 1,678,930 in 1916, and 580,853 in 1918.[17] August and September saw massive strikes centring on New South Wales, beginning with opposition to the introduction of Taylor punch-cards (aimed at increasing efficiency) in the railway workshops in Sydney and spreading to the mines and water-front until some 76,000 men were involved.

Hughes, determined to keep shipping moving and overseas markets supplied, enlisted strike-breaking volunteers under the War Precautions Act – among the ships taking on scratch crews were the first Commonwealth Shipping Line vessels to appear in Australian ports, loading some of the wheat Hughes had sold to Britain. The volunteers lived in tents on the Sydney Cricket Ground, dubbed by the strikers the 'Scabs Camping Ground'. Hughes defeated the strike, but there was much bitterness. It was in the aftermath of these strikes that the second conscription campaign was fought.

This time Hughes did his best to minimise the power of the anti-conscriptionists. The question put was about rein-forcements and did not mention conscription directly. In their speeches, Hughes and his colleagues made it clear that only sufficient men would be taken to raise the enlistment rate to 7,000 a month and then only single men. People of German background were prevented from voting. The vote was held on a weekday during working hours to reduce the working-class turnout. Soldiers were given the vote regardless of age (the fighting age was 18 and voting age 21). Censorship was exercised so rigorously that Ryan's Labor government in Queensland had to resort to reading Anti propaganda in the

House in order to get it published officially, though Hansard was eventually seized. Relations between Hughes and Ryan became so strained that Queensland police stood by when Hughes was pelted with rotten eggs at a meeting in Warwick, on the Queensland-New South Wales border, leading Hughes to finalise arrangements to found the federal police force to guard federal Members of Parliament, employees and property. More than eggs were thrown at many other meetings, including at a mass meeting of over 100,000 at the Melbourne Cricket Ground, where Hughes narrowly avoided serious injury when rocks were thrown at him. At the same meeting a man escaped capture after he was spotted about to throw a knife at the Prime Minister.[18]

Mannix, now Archbishop of Melbourne, and Ryan spoke to equally large meetings. Mannix had earlier in the year denounced the War as 'an ordinary trade war' (later misreported as a 'sordid trade war') rather than a defence of small nations (a veiled reference to Irish Home Rule made under the cloak of 'brave little Belgium'), and said Australia had done enough already. People should put 'Australia first, the Empire second.' Hughes found scapegoats in Sinn Fein and the IWW, attacking Mannix, for example, as an alien Sinn Feiner hellbent on *sowing the seeds of discord amongst the Australian people*, who would set *class against class, creed against creed* and *make Australia a pawn in the game of fanning the feuds of the old world*.[19]

The result was a larger 'No' majority, at 166,588, and of the states only Victoria changed (to 'No'). The soldiers still voted 'Yes' but by an even smaller margin than the first time, with those at the Front voting 'No'. Hughes tendered his resignation, as he had promised to do if he lost, but this was not accepted by the Governor-General and he was reappointed

Prime Minister as he still commanded the majority in the House. In France, the AIF was given higher proportions of Lewis guns and tanks to compensate for anticipated shortages of men; the German offensive was arrested at Villers Bretonneux in the spring of 1918; and an Australian, Major-General John Monash, was appointed army commander. Victories at the Battles of Hamel, Peronne and Mont St Quentin ensued in the summer.

The enviable Anzac reputation, forged at Gallipoli and in Palestine, was enhanced in France and Belgium. Hughes had been a divisive figure domestically, but as the principal civilian supporter of the AIF and with a freshly-minted and telling nickname, 'the Little Digger', he had forged a new and lasting constituency among the AIF and its families. Their sacrifice would inspire him in his quest for a just peace for Australia.

The Canadians had been a separate Corps since September 1915 and their Corps came under Canadian command in the person of Lieutenant General Sir Arthur Currie in June 1917 after their great success in the Battle of Vimy Ridge. The Canadian Corps also had a completely separate civil administration from the start. It functioned as a national army. The AIF, in contrast, was much more integrated into the British Army, though it increasingly followed the Canadian example. Hughes argued unsuccessfully for an ANZAC Army in March 1916. The AIF was first organised into an Australian Corps under a British general, Sir William Birdwood, in October 1917; it finally got an Australian commander with John Monash's appointment in May 1918.

5

Man of Empire, 1918

In the domestic political travails of 1917 Hughes had found it impossible to leave Australia for London and the first round of meetings of Lloyd George's so-called Imperial War Cabinet. He thus missed the impact of Jan Smuts, the South African Defence Minister, who made a name for himself trying to broker a position between Woodrow Wilson's international idealism, fully enunciated later in Wilson's Fourteen Points of 8 January 1918, and British and French realism. In April 1918 Hughes sailed for Britain for the next round. On Murdoch's advice, he did so via the United States, where he planned to make the sort of barn-storming speeches that had made such an impression on the British public two years earlier. Writing to the Governor-General on the eve of his departure – fortuitously it was Anzac Day and the day the AIF stemmed the German tide at Villers Bretonneux – he was candid about his feelings: *I'm sorrier than I can say to leave Australia. I love this country but I feel it my duty to go.*[1]

Hughes did not know it at the time, but he would be away from Australia for an extraordinary and unprecedented 15 months. He took with him his wife and young daughter, his conservative colleague Joseph Cook as co-delegate, Robert Garran as his official secretary, and John Latham, a young naval reservist and Melbourne lawyer with expertise in Pacific intelligence matters, as Cook's secretary. There were also Percy Deane, Hughes' personal assistant, Dr R Mungovan his physician, two typists and a messenger. Another Melbourne lawyer Frederic Eggleston and Captain Henry Gullett, the delegation's press officer, joined them later on; as did Keith Murdoch, who was always at hand but never part of the official party; and W S Robinson, who acted as an unofficial trade adviser. In his inimitable way, Hughes would sideline his despised former opponent Cook from most important matters for the whole trip, but would also reward him with a knighthood to keep him quiet.

David Low of the *Bulletin* expressed something of the Australian national mood when he published a fantastic and satirical, though fairly sympathetic, cartoon booklet, *The Billy Book: Hughes Abroad*, as the party sailed.[2] In it Hughes appears as a diminutive cross between Charlie Chaplin and an ancestor of Bazza McKenzie, a canny innocent thrust into cosmopolitan society who had a knack of coming out on top or at least surviving with his sense of humour intact. Low's book also features a toy, the Billiwog, 'London's latest craze', 'Almost Human', 'Babies Cry for it', 'No war is complete without one': a red-faced, screaming Billy with scrawny arms aloft. 'Directions for use – Blow up with wind until head expands, then release hole in face, whereupon Billy will emit loud noises until he goes flat.'[3] The book was a runaway success and sold 60,000 copies.[4] Hughes, to his credit, took it all in the jocular spirit in which it was intended.

Hughes and his party made landfall at Vancouver on 19 May and immediately crossed the border to Seattle, where ten wooden ships were being built for the Australian government. Progress was good: three had already been launched and a fourth would be the next day. He also arranged to see some concrete ships and enlisted an expert on these to visit Australia with a view to constructing them there under license.[5] He then proceeded to Washington where he saw senior officials and gained an exemption from a United States ban on the export of steel plates which were needed for shipbuilding in Australia.[6]

On 29 May Hughes was taken by Lord Reading, the British Ambassador to the United States, to meet Woodrow Wilson. Reading reported to London: 'Mr Hughes impressed upon the President that it was vital to the security of Australia that Germany should never be allowed to take any part of New Guinea or the Islands of the Pacific. Mr Hughes made plain that Australia was not seeking all these islands for herself[,] that she had sufficient territory[,] but that her life would be menaced if Germany with her predatory designs held any of these Islands[,] and he emphasised the necessity of these belonging only to the British Empire and friendly Powers.'[7]

Wilson's reply was totally non-committal, though he knew as well as Hughes did that Hughes was really referring to delimiting Japanese influence in the Pacific. Hughes' account in his memoirs is more graphic than Reading's: *President Wilson received me courteously and when after a few non-committal words I ventured to set out the views of the Government of the Commonwealth [of Australia] on the future of the islands of the Pacific, he heard me in silence, listening intently to all I said, but remaining as unresponsive as the Sphinx in the desert.*[8]

Clearly the President would need to be persuaded. Afterwards, Hughes was allowed to meet Wilson's expert advisers, the so-called Inquiry, who were preparing preliminary briefings for the Peace Conference which would follow the War, but they were equally silent.[9] Murdoch had told Hughes, who did not need telling, that he 'would have trouble with Wilson over the German Pacific islands if there is no propaganda'.[10] To this end, Hughes made a major speech to the Anglophile businessmen and professionals of the Pilgrims Club in New York on 1 June.

Hughes began by saying that *I stand among friends* and proclaimed it a *great day* when the United States had *deliberately entered the arena of war* at a time when *the fate of Civilisation hangs by a hair*. The vibrant young democracy of the United States offered an *inspiration* to Australia both in peace and war. *Australia looks to you, her elder brother, to stand by her around the peace table as well as on the field of battle*. He then called for *an Australasian Monroe Doctrine for the South Pacific*. (William Massey, the New Zealand Prime Minister, had crossed the Pacific with Hughes on the same ship and had agreed with his position.)

Warming to his theme, Hughes continued. Infected by *evil doctrines*, Germany wanted to *encircle with her hairy arms the entire world*. He feared a *so-called Peace* that would be a *reign of terror* for Australia, which would be *awaiting the next swoop of the vulture* should Germany keep possession of New Guinea, which stood on Australia's doorstep as the Channel ports did to Britain, or Cuba or Hawaii did to the continental United States: *to allow another nation to control them* [New Guinea and adjacent islands] *would be to allow it to control Australia*. Australia had occupied German New Guinea at the start of the War, and *what we have we hold. We do not desire Empire, but only security*, he concluded, security *against all predatory nations*.[11]

Hughes next met the Association of Foreign Correspondents in America at the Harvard Club. To them he explained Australia's root-and-branch attitude to excluding German trading and financial interests, and he reiterated his call for an Australasian Monroe Doctrine. These two meetings cast down the gauntlet to Wilson in no uncertain terms. His American visit convinced Hughes that Australia needed direct representation in the United States: trade representatives in New York and on the West Coast, and a diplomatic representative in Washington. He wrote to Acting Prime Minister W A Watt: *The British Embassy of course acts for us in a casual sort of way, but you know what Englishmen are. They haven't the remotest idea of what Australia is like nor of its importance, and even with the best of intentions they are unsatisfactory. The only British representative here [in New York] is the Consul General. He is positively too dreadful for words.*[12] Consequently, Henry Braddon, from the great wool company Dalgety, was appointed Australian Commissioner to the United States for two years, based in New York and with a commercial brief.[13] Hughes then crossed the Atlantic in a British cruiser, arriving in London on 15 June.

'We do not desire Empire, but only security against all predatory nations.'
BILLY HUGHES, 1 JUNE 1918

Living in a house provided by the British government in Hampstead, he set about picking up the loose ends left after his 1916 visit. There were three main strands: serving on the Imperial War Cabinet; public speaking in favour of Empire trade and making Germany pay; and negotiating more deals for selling Australian primary products to Britain. The three were inter-connected.

Of the Imperial War Cabinet, which met nearly every day in June and July and less frequently in the ensuing months, he observed that *the Dominion Prime Ministers, but lately complaining that they had been kept in the dark, were dazzled by the fierce glare that now beat upon them. But yesterday they had known nothing; now, alas! They knew everything, and their last state was worse than the first.*[14]

In the Imperial Cabinet with his peers, Hughes argued for an increase in technology (aeroplanes, tanks and artillery) as a means of winning the War and of compensating for declining Imperial manpower (though Lloyd George pointed out that the United States had promised 120 Divisions). Monash's copybook all-arms victory at Hamel on 4 July bore this out, as did the rolling back of the German offensive more widely leading to the 'Black Day' of the German Army when it faced defeat at the

> In the Treaty of Brest-Litovsk, signed on 3 March 1918, Russia ceded 30 per cent of its territory, including nine-tenths of its coal mines, to the German and Turkish spheres and, in a subsequent financial agreement of 27 August, agreed to pay an indemnity of 6 billion marks.

Battle of Amiens on 8 August. This military success seemed a vindication of Hughes's decision in May to appoint Monash to command the ANZAC Corps. Hughes would long bask in the memory of his fleeting dash across the Channel to visit his beloved Diggers and Monash on the eve of Hamel.

Hughes supported calls for direct access to the British Prime Minister by the Dominion Prime Ministers but opposed Smuts's plans for Imperial federation. Australia's Parliament had to remain sovereign, in his view. He also supported a proposed, but never realised, Japanese-United States military intervention into far-eastern Russia. Most of all, Hughes advocated a strong line with Germany over trade, colonies and reparations. Had not the Germans themselves imposed a Carthaginian treaty on the Russians at Brest-Litovsk?

He argued that the British Empire should oppose Wilson's

PRESIDENT WILSON'S FOURTEEN POINTS, 8 JANUARY 1918

The program of the world's peace, therefore, is our program; and that program, the only possible program, as we see it, is this:

I. Open covenants of peace, openly arrived at, after which there shall be no private international understandings of any kind but diplomacy shall proceed always frankly and in the public view.

II. Absolute freedom of navigation upon the seas, outside territorial waters, alike in peace and in war, except as the seas may be closed in whole or in part by international action for the enforcement of international covenants.

III. The removal, so far as possible, of all economic barriers and the establishment of an equality of trade conditions among all the nations consenting to the peace and associating themselves for its maintenance.

IV. Adequate guarantees given and taken that national armaments will be reduced to the lowest point consistent with domestic safety.

V. A free, open-minded, and absolutely impartial adjustment of all colonial claims, based upon a strict observance of the principle that in determining all such questions of sovereignty the interests of the populations concerned must have equal weight with the equitable claims of the government whose title is to be determined.

VI. The evacuation of all Russian territory and such a settlement of all questions affecting Russia as will secure the best and freest cooperation of the other nations of the world in obtaining for her an unhampered and unembarrassed opportunity for the independent determination of her own political development and national policy and assure her of a sincere welcome into the society of free nations under institutions of her own choosing; and, more than a welcome, assistance also of every kind that she may need and may herself desire. The treatment accorded Russia by her sister nations in the months to come will be the acid test of their good will, of their comprehension of her needs as distinguished from their own interests, and of their intelligent and unselfish sympathy.

VII. Belgium, the whole world will agree, must be evacuated and restored, without any attempt to limit the sovereignty which she enjoys in common with all other free nations. No other single act will serve as this will serve to restore confidence among the nations in the laws which they have themselves set and determined for the government of their relations with one another. Without this healing act the whole structure and validity of international law is forever impaired.

VIII. All French territory should be freed and the invaded portions restored, and the wrong done to France by Prussia in 1871 in the matter of Alsace-Lorraine, which has unsettled the peace of the world for nearly fifty years, should be righted, in order that peace may once more be made secure in the interest of all.

IX. A readjustment of the frontiers of Italy should be effected along clearly recognizable lines of nationality.

X. The peoples of Austria-Hungary, whose place among the nations we wish to see safeguarded and assured, should be accorded the freest opportunity to autonomous development.

XI. Rumania, Serbia, and Montenegro should be evacuated; occupied territories restored; Serbia accorded free and secure access to the sea; and the relations of the several Balkan states to one another determined by friendly counsel along historically established lines of allegiance and nationality; and international guarantees of the political and economic independence and territorial integrity of the several Balkan states should be entered into.

XII. The Turkish portion of the present Ottoman Empire should be assured a secure sovereignty, but the other nationalities which are now under Turkish rule should be assured an undoubted security of life and an absolutely unmolested opportunity of autonomous development, and the Dardanelles should be permanently opened as a free passage to the ships and commerce of all nations under international guarantees.

XIII. An independent Polish state should be erected which should include the territories inhabited by indisputably Polish populations, which should be assured a free and secure access to the sea, and whose political and economic independence and territorial integrity should be guaranteed by international covenant.

XIV. A general association of nations must be formed under specific covenants for the purpose of affording mutual guarantees of political independence and territorial integrity to great and small states alike.

Fourteen Points as the basis for peace talks, particularly the calls for no annexations, reparations or indemnities, for the so-called 'freedom of the seas', and for a utopian League of Nations which would outlaw war. First settle the peace terms and only then talk about a League of Nations. He did not want Britain to commit the Empire 'irrevocably' to peace terms in *'pourparleys'* before he and Massey could arrive in London to influence them. All of Wilson's views cut across ideas for Imperial preference, Imperial defence, the annexation of the German Pacific colonies, paying for the War, and the protection of White Australia. On New Guinea, Hughes said bluntly: *If you want to shift us, come and do it: here we are − J'y suis, j'y reste.*[15]

The public propaganda campaign began with a speech to the British Empire Producers Association in the Queen's Hall, London, on 10 July. Do not listen to *the babble of talk from visionaries and doctrinaires*, he said in a thinly veiled reference to Wilson. Before the War the British Empire had lost out to Germany because the Empire's *laissez faire* free trade could not match Germany's national policy. German *national* commercial strategy had led to Germany's gaining control of much of the world's raw materials, including those necessary to wage war, and by *peaceful penetration* Germany had *honeycomb*[ed] *the commercial and industrial life of Britain*. Britain needed guaranteed raw materials from loyal Imperial suppliers, like Australia. The Empire's workers had *fought and bled* for the country; they deserved leaders who *treated the Empire in a business-like way* ... [and] *understand what is necessary and are not afraid to do it*. Germany should have a *Brest-Litovsk* visited upon itself.[16]

Over the next six weeks or so, and despite suffering a bout of Spanish flu, Hughes criss-crossed the country, making speeches propagating these views. In some he named Henry Merton and Company, the German metal combine's British arm, as the main offender (or Germany's *blood brother* in his terms), nourishing Germany by sucking wealth out of the British economy. His remarks got under the skin of the Liberal Party, which held free trade as a shibboleth. This was a risky strategy as the Liberals were Lloyd George's own party and a key element in the coalition government. Merton had 'naturalised' its board after war had broken out, so they sued Hughes for libel, and eventually won in March 1920 in an out-of-court settlement which cost the Australian government £6,500. Unsurprisingly, Hughes's press reception during this visit was more mixed, as he was perceived to be driving a wedge between the coalition partners, and the crusade was abandoned in early September.[17] However, his friend, Walter Long, the Tory Colonial Secretary, could still write to him that his speeches 'are like a fine bracing breeze that invigorates us all'.[18]

Though the other Dominion Prime Ministers returned home in mid-August, Hughes felt he had to stay behind, partly to make up for ground lost by his absence from London in 1917, to look after the interests of the AIF, and mostly to push on with the sale of vital Australian products. By badgering the Shipping Controller, Hughes eventually found places on Australia-bound ships to give 7,500 of the original Gallipoli Anzacs home leave. On commodity sales, Hughes wrote on 28 September to Munro Ferguson: *I pass laborious and fretful days, going round and round like a clockwork mouse. However I'll sell the wheat copper lead butter tallow hides etc. I must do so for without money we cannot finance the war.*[19]

Wheat was the most difficult, as even with the

THE MOUSE AND WEEVIL PLAGUES OF 1917–18
As Australian wheat was stored in hessian bags and stacked at railway sidings, it proved a huge temptation for mice, which had multiplied to plague proportions by the middle of 1917. On 1 June an official of the Victorian Vermin Destruction Department reported 13 tons of mice destroyed at eight railway stations. One letter to a newspaper described the mice chewing boots, bedding, paper, clothing, even the cork from the tops of bottles. 'If we kill one, a hundred come to its funeral. We pick up from 1,000 to 2,000 every day. We have got tired of counting them, so we measure them by the bucket – about 500 to the bucket.'[20] Stacks were soon protected with half-buried sheets of galvanised iron bent outwards. Next there came a massive weevil infestation, itself to be controlled by the simple expedient of interrupting the insect's life cycle by sanitising the soil around wheat stacks.[21] Much of the wheat, thus protected, had to wait until the shipping shortage eased after the War before it could be sent to Britain.

Commonwealth Shipping Line ships it was impossible to move much of it to Britain. Of the 3 million tons Hughes had sold to the British government in 1916 (nearly three-quarters of the 1916–17 season's crop) at the good price of 5s per bushel (1 ton is 39.375 bushels), two-thirds had still not got to Britain by mid 1918, though the British government had paid for it. Nevertheless, the British agreed to buy the 1917–18 crop (1.5 million tons), but only if almost all of the ships in the Australian coastal trade, including those of the Commonwealth Shipping Line (47 in all) came under British control. Hughes held out and the purchase was finally agreed without the shipping stipulation in July 1919 after the War had ended. Though it had been unclear in 1916, by 1918 the British Treasury concluded with justification that the deals, as with some for other commodities, were not in Britain's economic interest but were undertaken 'on [the] higher political grounds' of keeping Australia in business during the War.

To the lasting benefit of Australian wheat farmers, the astute Hughes had realised this and acted accordingly.[22]

Wool, sold to the British government for the duration of the War, was an easier proposition. The agreement ran until 1920 and a follow-up until 1924; and although world wool prices skyrocketed well above the originally agreed price, under the agreements half of the profits from the resale of the surplus of Britain's purchase went back to the Australian growers, realising some £40 million profit by that time. Hides and tallow, as essential war materials (yielding leather for belts, boots, saddles and harness in the former case and glycerine for the cordite in munitions in the latter) were easy to dispose of; likewise, lead and zinc. Copper, however, was in oversupply and the British had to be persuaded to support that industry for political reasons. Meat, jam, cheese and butter readily found their way into military rations. Despite the endemic shipping crisis, Australia's exports overall grew from £79 million in 1913 to £114 million in 1918. Hughes was delivering the goods and thereby satisfying key elements of his electoral base.[23]

Weighing up the impact of the War on Australia's economy, scholars have noted that under the enforced protection of the shipping crisis and the cutting off of enemy supplies, domestic manufacturing, mostly textile mills, grew by a quarter. One graphic example was Melbourne pharmaceutical manufacturer Alfred Nicholas, whose painkiller Aspro replaced the German Bayer Aspirin in Australia and later internationally – inevitably, Nicholas's mansion was christened 'Headache Hall'. Under Hughes' watchful tutelage, Broken Hill Proprietary opened its steel mill in Newcastle (New South Wales) in 1915 and expanded Hoskins mill in Lithgow (New South Wales). Broken Hill Associated Smelters began silver-lead smelting in Port Pirie (South Australia), took over a former German smelter at Port Kembla (New South Wales), and started a new zinc smelting works at Risdon (Tasmania). Much of this was controlled by Hughes' Melbourne business friends W S Robinson, W L Baillieu and F C Howard, and what came to be known as the Collins House Group. It was calculated officially in 1921 that Australians were on average 22 per cent richer than they were in 1915, or, when inflation is taken into account, 4 per cent richer. The War, despite all of its horrors, thus proved itself on balance to be of some material benefit to the surviving generation.[24]

By early October, spearheaded in part by the AIF, the Allies had broken the Hindenburg Line, General Sir Edmund Allenby's forces, including the Australian Light Horse, were in Damascus and Bulgaria had surrendered. The end of the War was now in sight and the Imperial War Cabinet began to discuss Armistice terms. Luckily for Hughes, Monash's AIF was playing a major role; ironically, the War would end before the troops conscription might have provided would have been needed.

On 12–15 October Hughes was briefly in Paris to receive the Grand Cross of the *Legion d'Honneur*. While there he met the Prime Minister Georges Clemenceau, various other Ministers and Marshal Ferdinand Foch the Allied Commander-in-Chief. He found that Clemenceau's Cabinet shared his views about annexations, reparations and a harsh peace; and he learned from Foch that he expected peace in six weeks. He reported the encounter in a cable to Watt in Melbourne: *I agree with Cabinet that I must stay here. It would be wrong for me to leave shortly, as I had intended soon after I had sold our products. Terms of peace will affect future of world, of Empire, of Commonwealth, and these terms will, in effect, be settled long before formal peace conference meets – in fact they are in process of being settled now. I had conference with several Ministers French War Cabinet, as well as with Clemenceau, and discussed Wilson's fourteen points. They think as I do. I strongly urged them to let the voice of France be heard. The people of Britain and France are very determined that the fruits of victory shall not be taken away from them by trickery. There will probably be 24 or maybe 64 points before we have done. Some of the original fourteen, inter alia two, three and five [that is, freedom of the seas, no tariff barriers and no annexations] , will wholly disappear or be so changed that no one will know them … It is rumoured that Germany has surrendered unconditionally.*[25]

> **'Terms of peace will affect future of world, of Empire, of Commonwealth, and these terms will, in effect, be settled long before formal peace conference meets – in fact they are in process of being settled now.'**
>
> **BILLY HUGHES, 16 OCTOBER 1918**

A few days later, he wrote again to Watt: *I feel that there are powerful influences working assiduously beneath the surface for Peace other than a dictated Peace … [T]o speak quite candidly as I see things British Party Politics ignore Imperial Interest. There is no Imperial Government in this great crisis although there may be an Imperial War Cabinet … I am trying to do what I can to hold up Australia's end here, and to prevent any peace that does not guarantee peace of world and safeguard our interests in Pacific and elsewhere.*[26] Hughes was preparing himself for the political battle of his life. Thinking of himself as a better Briton than his Imperial compatriots in the Mother Country, he would remind them of where their true interests lay.

Unknown to Hughes, Lloyd George, who was looking to

appease Wilson, had engineered a series of British Cabinet meetings to discuss the Armistice terms and Hughes would not be invited to attend. Hughes, therefore, blithely set out on a speaking tour of the north of England. The British Cabinet authorised Lloyd George to go forthwith to Paris to the Inter-Allied Council and agreed to base the Armistice on the Fourteen Points save for reservations about 'freedom of the seas' and 'restoration', meaning reparations. Annexations and tariff regimes were to be left for another occasion. This became the Allied position.

Returning to be confronted by this *fait accompli*, a slighted and very angry Hughes made a public speech and wrote a letter to *The Times* complaining that the Dominions had not been consulted.[27] Three days later, to great jubilation, the War ended; but Hughes still felt he had no satisfactory answers to his questions. In the next meetings of the Imperial War Cabinet and in letters to Lloyd George, he raised the issues of lack of consultation, of the peace terms, and specifically the Pacific Islands question and Dominions representation at the forthcoming Paris Peace Conference.

In the Imperial War Cabinet on 5 November Hughes made it clear that, *Speaking for himself, he declined to be bound to the chariot-wheel of the Fourteen Points, particularly that dealing with the League of Nations. He would not be party to a League of Nations until he knew exactly what was meant by it*.[28] Lloyd George said that having the Fourteen Points as a basis for discussion did not mean that they had to be agreed to as the final terms. Hughes would later explain that his fears about the League were related to his insistence that Australia should control its own immigration policy, tariffs and defence arrangements: *No country would allow its vital interests to be decided by anyone except itself*. Rather than have a *world-State* he thought the *best solution would be an agreement between the United States and Great Britain, which would ensure the peace of the world.*[29] He feared that Wilson, whose country had made *no money sacrifice at all* wanted to be *the god in the machine* at the peace talks, and argued that Lloyd George, fresh from his strong mandate in the General Election on 14 December, should stand up to Wilson. Lloyd George replied that the British Empire would have its due but that 'the League of Nations was to him [Wilson] what a toy was to a child – he would not be happy until he got it'.[30]

In an early discussion on reparations, Hughes made the point that Germany should pay the full cost of the Allies' War, estimated at £300 million for Australia; and Lloyd George replied tellingly that by selling goods in the international market the German economy had to be allowed to trade its way into a position to be able to pay reparations. If total war debts were paid, German workers would be 'slaves' for 'two generations' and an army of occupation would be required for enforcement of the terms. The estimated amount Germany could afford to pay was £2,000 million per annum, far short of the £100,000 million Britain alone owed the United States. As a trading nation, Britain needed a prosperous Germany to buy its goods. This pragmatic 'free trade' view was quite contrary to Hughes's doctrinaire Imperial protectionist one.[31] A pre-occupation with immediate spoils, it appears, blinded him to Australia's wider interest in a prosperous Britain; or, perhaps, he was intent on arguing his sectional case knowing full well that Lloyd George would get most of what he wanted on the wider issue.

Lloyd George appointed a Committee on Indemnity, cleverly making Hughes its chairman, and added Canada's Finance Minister, and four from Britain (the Colonial Secretary, a former Director of the Bank of England, an academic economist and a merchant banker). They were instructed to report on Germany's capacity to pay, the method of payment and the likely effect on the receiving nations, and to do so before the British general election due on 14 December. After interviewing John Maynard Keynes from the Treasury and senior Board of Trade officials, and taking written submissions, they conjured up a guesstimate of £24,000 million for the total amount and an annual payment of £1,200 million which they thought Germany could well afford. Armed with the report on 10 December, on the eve of the election, Lloyd George made a speech in Bristol saying Britain would 'demand the whole cost of the war' and that an expert committee had calculated that 'it can be done'.

With the election safely won, however, and Lloyd George's immediate purpose realised, the Imperial War Cabinet on 24 December watered down its instructions to its Paris delegation, asking them 'to secure from Germany the greatest possible indemnity she can pay consistently with the economic well-being of the British Empire and the peace of the world, and without involving an army of occupation'.[32] The Treasury had estimated the reparations bill for Germany as low as £3,000 million and the Board of Trade £2,000 million.[33] The Canadian on Hughes' committee later wrote in his memoirs: 'Altogether it was the oddest committee I ever served upon', relying on impressions and wishful thinking rather than evidence, keen 'to make the Hun pay to the utmost, whether it leads to a generation of occupancy and direction, or not, and forgetful of the results otherwise'.[34]

Amery, an Empire-minded British Conservative MP sympathetic to Hughes, wrote to Smuts about the indemnity issue at this time: 'Old Hughes isn't getting up on his hind legs without some justification.' Australian cities and countryside may not have suffered direct war damage but Australian trade had been severely disrupted and the nation had not profited from the War. And he added perceptively: 'even if we [the British Empire] don't get the actual compensation we ought to in money, it may make the situation much easier for us as regards our territorial claims.' [35]

On the Pacific Islands, prompted by a Japanese official statement claiming the islands north of the Equator, Hughes (no doubt relying on Latham's expert advice) wrote confidentially to Lloyd George outlining in detail the strategic reasons why the Japanese should be denied. The main base at Truk in the Carolines was closer to Townsville than to Yokohama. Sailing time from Japanese territory to Australia would be more than halved and with it the potential military threat doubled.[36] In the Imperial War Cabinet meetings, Lloyd George reiterated that it was the Empire's policy to hold on to the former German territories it had occupied, but that it had to honour its 1915 secret agreement with Japan (confirmed formally in 1917) to allow the Japanese to occupy those territories it had taken north of the Equator. Hughes said that Australia had never accepted that position and reserved his right to argue the point for Australia at the Peace Conference. In fact, Fisher in 1915 and Hughes in 1917 had reluctantly accepted the position subject to the proviso that it would be discussed *de novo* at the peace talks after the War.[37]

On the thorny matter of the Dominions' representation at the Peace Conference, Sir Robert Borden, the Canadian Prime Minister, led the charge by insisting on separate representation, a view endorsed by the other Dominion leaders. This annoyed the French and Americans who did not want what they saw as an inflated British representation. Ultimately a compromise was reached whereby the Dominions were given the same representation as small nations (two delegates each for Canada, Australia, South Africa and India; one for New Zealand; and Newfoundland would be represented by the British Empire delegation generally). Each Dominion would be entitled to make separate representations when their specific interests were under discussion, but otherwise the Dominion representatives would each occupy in turn a single 'Empire' position on the British Empire delegation. Hughes and his Imperial colleagues had to be satisfied with this as the best deal they could get.[38]

Throughout the robust in-the-family discussions of 1918 Hughes demonstrated again and again that Imperial loyalty was as much a practical tool to use as it was a mere manifestation of sentiment. He had even dabbled once more in British domestic politics to useful effect. He would go to the Peace Conference as a representative of both Australia and the British Empire. Having the Empire behind him would amplify his voice and make it heard in a way it never would have been had Australia been reliant solely on its own resources.

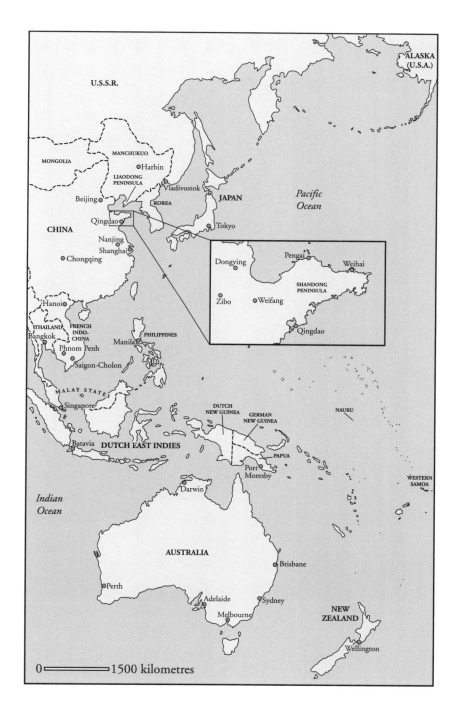

The Australian premier William Hughes inspects an Anzac guard of honour in
London 1918.

II

The Paris Peace Conference

6
Peacemaking, 1919

The Paris Peace Conference proper opened on 18 January with a formal plenary session in the Salle d'Horloge at the Quai d'Orsay attended by representatives of all 32 countries. Always aware of symbolical symmetries, Clemenceau reversed the outcome of the Franco-Prussian War by choosing the anniversary of the proclamation of the German Empire in 1871. The Conference would last nearly six gruelling months until the Treaty with Germany was signed in the Hall of Mirrors at Versailles, again reflecting 1871, on 28 June.

The *modus operandi* of the Conference was that the old Supreme War Council continued as the Council of Ten (the leaders of the United States, Britain, France, Italy and Japan and their Foreign Ministers) as a cabinet-style body, which in practice became the Council of Four (leaders of all minus Japan) or Three (when Italy withdrew over a territorial claim at Fiume). There were also occasional plenary sessions and a range of Commissions set up to report on specific issues such as the League of Nations and reparations.

In addition, each delegation had its own round of meetings, which might be quite complex, as was the case for the

14-strong British Empire delegation. It was, of course, in the nucleus of this atom, the Council of Four, that the real political activity took place. Satellites from the outer orbits, like Hughes, were occasionally admitted to petition this body on matters which specifically concerned them, such as New Guinea or the Racial Equality Clause (impinging on the White Australia policy). Hughes also played a role as one of the three British Empire delegates on and Deputy Chairman of the Reparations Commission, which had 29 members.

Australia, through Hughes, was concerned principally with three specific issues: New Guinea and the other formerly German Pacific islands south of the Equator, racial equality and reparations. It was also concerned more generally with such issues as the proposed League of Nations, freedom of the seas, tariff restrictions, German disarmament and occupation forces. In rough chronology, the colonies came first, then racial equality, then reparations and finally the League. The first two issues will be discussed in this chapter and the other two in the next.

Hughes spelled out the advantage of his dual status as both an Australian and a British Empire delegate in a reflection published in 1929: *Although technically the status of the Dominions and India was no higher than the status of the score of smaller nations which waited about with little information and even less influence while the four or five Great Powers decided, in actual fact they were included in the deciding Powers, for, by virtue of their membership of the British delegation, they formulated the policy which their spokesman, the Prime Minister of the United Kingdom, advocated in the Council of Four. They were kept in touch with all that went on; they were able to express their views at every stage. On many of the important commissions on which the Great*

Powers were represented, the representative of the British Empire was a Dominion Minister, and no important step was taken except after discussion and agreement at the British Empire Delegation. Thus the right of the self-governing parts of the Empire to an effective voice in foreign affairs, recognised by the British during the war, was fully exercised at the Peace Conference.[1] This is a somewhat idealised view, but it was certainly the case that the Imperial connection magnified the Australian voice and, in important matters of concern to Australia, the British world spoke as one.

So it was on colonies. The Fourteen Points prescribed 'no annexations' whereas Australia, South Africa and New Zealand wished to keep the German colonial territories that they had occupied early in the War: New Guinea, South-West Africa and Samoa. Each colony was close to the respective Dominion's borders and, in the Australian and New Zealand cases, of great strategic importance. (Japan had a similar claim over the Pacific islands north of the Equator and with Shandong on the Chinese mainland.) President Wilson was attracted to an idea first canvassed by Smuts in a paper written before the Conference which suggested that the former Ottoman territories in the Middle East should be held in trust by member states as 'Mandates' of the new League of Nations, reporting regularly on progress towards self-government. Smuts was horrified when the Americans suggested that South-West Africa and the Pacific islands should also be Mandated. He believed that countries such as Syria, Mesopotamia and Palestine were sufficiently civilised to become democracies in time, but much of Africa and the Pacific were too 'primitive' to achieve this outcome in any foreseeable future.

On 24 and 25 January, on Lloyd George's initiative, the

Dominion Prime Ministers, including Sir Robert Borden of Canada who was present for moral support, addressed the Council of Ten. Clemenceau is reported to have said to Lloyd George 'Bring your savages with you,' and to add in the meeting, 'Mr 'ughes. I have 'eard that in early life you were a cannibal,' to which Hughes replied, *that has been greatly exaggerated*.[2]

Using a large map of the Pacific with Australia at its centre, especially prepared by the Royal Geographical Society in London, Hughes pointed out on the first day that *the islands encompassed Australia like fortresses*; and on the second that, *As Ireland is to the United Kingdom, as Mexico is to the United States, as Alsace-Lorraine is to France, so is New Guinea to Australia*. Wilson replied on 27 January with a story about a man who kept buying real estate because he could not bear the thought of anyone owning land adjacent to his own, and said the attitude was 'based on a fundamental lack of faith in the League of Nations'. Any attack on a Mandate, he said, and the League would retaliate, 'with the United States in the lead'. His private thinking, however, was less idealistic. In a pencilled note on a secret, background memorandum supplied by his adviser Colonel Edward House, Wilson had written: 'My difficulty is with the demands of men like Hughes and the certain difficulties with Japan. The latter loom large. A line of islands in her possession would be very dangerous to the U.S.'[3] Plainly Wilson was keen to have Mandates imposed more as a means of circumventing the Japanese than of controlling the activities of the Dominions. In subsequent meetings the French, saying that they agreed with Hughes, wanted to annex the Cameroons and Togoland, and the Japanese put their claims. A split with the United States was imminent.[4] Lord Eustace Percy, of the British

Empire delegation, noted that the Mandates idea 'seemed in danger of splitting on the rock of South African and Australian nationalism'.[5] He should have added French, Italian and Japanese nationalism to boot. According to an article by Murdoch in the Melbourne *Herald*, not an unimpeachable source but this time with more than a grain of truth, Clemenceau whispered to Hughes after he spoke, 'You made a strong case,' and Vittorio Orlando, the Italian Prime Minister, added, 'You made out our case for Dalmatia'.[6] Hughes 'is being used as a catspaw by the French', Eggleston fulminated in his private diary,[7] but he failed to observe that Hughes was being used knowingly and it was to his and his allies' mutual advantage. Perhaps, at another level, it was ultimately to Wilson's too.

Concerned about the impasse, the British Empire delegation strove to overcome it. Inspired principally by Smuts, Latham, Clement Jones and Loring Christie (Latham's British and Canadian equivalents) on 29 January came up with a formula for a new, third class of Mandate, 'C' class, which for all intents and purposes would be annexed territories. 'C' class Mandates, they wrote, 'owing to the sparseness of their population and small size, or their remoteness from the centres of civilisation, or their geographical contiguity to the Mandatory State, and other circumstances, can be best administered under the laws of the Mandatory State as integral portions thereof, subject to the safeguards above mentioned [reporting to the League] in the interests of the indigenous population.'[8]

This was crucial for Hughes, as it gave Australia control of immigration into New Guinea, thereby allowing him to keep the Japanese out. Australia would determine tariffs, wages and so on. Mandatories would also be prohibited from fortifying the Mandates. Australia could not militarise its new islands; but, crucially, neither could Japan its acquired territories. Sir Maurice Hankey, Secretary to the British Cabinet and the Peace Conference, mollified Hughes, who alone had been holding out for annexation, by reassuring him that the 'C' class Mandate was 'the equivalent of a 999 years' lease'.[9]

In the heated debate within the British Empire delegation, Lloyd George is reported to have lost his temper with Hughes, saying that he 'would not quarrel with the United States for the Solomon Islands,' and that he would not send the Royal Navy to defend Australia if he persisted in his views. Hughes is reported to have replied that he would *go to England and ask the people who own the Navy what they have to say about it*. Hughes said that if an *open door* applied in New Guinea regarding trade and migration then he feared *the territory would become a Japanese or a Japanese and German country within ten years*. Given his rudimentary Welsh and Lloyd George's fluency in that language, Hughes's story that the two men continued in Welsh is patently an exaggeration. Later, doubtless with a glint in his eye, Lloyd George told Amery he would not be intimidated by 'a damned little Welshman'.[10] At this stage Hughes, it appears, totally or partly, inspired an article in the Paris edition of the *Daily Mail*, containing direct quotes from the confidential Council of Ten meeting and an allegation that Lloyd George was favouring Wilson's woolly-minded idealism over the legitimate claims of the Dominions. An incandescent Wilson threatened to go home.

At the next meeting of the Council of Ten, Wilson determined to put Hughes and Massey (of New Zealand), who had also been holding out, in their places. The meeting began with a speech by Hughes which accepted the 'C' class

Mandate compromise. As the transcript solemnly noted: *Australia fully recognised that grave interests, involving the fate of humanity were at stake and, therefore, he did not feel justified in opposing the views of President Wilson and those of Mr Lloyd George, beyond the point which may reasonably safeguard the interests of Australia.*[11] But Wilson, smarting over the *Daily Mail* attack, wanted his pound of flesh. Egos were on the line, so he chose not to listen. Were they, he said, presenting an 'ultimatum'? 'Am I to understand that if the whole civilized world asks Australia to agree to a mandate for these islands, Australia is prepared to defy the opinion of the whole civilized world?' Hughes, perhaps pretending that his hearing apparatus was malfunctioning, hesitated and replied calmly, *That's about the size of it Mr President.* Returning to the charge, Wilson asked whether he thought five million Australians should hold to ransom the 1,200 million represented by the Conference. Hughes replied, devastatingly, *I represent sixty thousand [war] dead*, which as all present knew was more than Wilson did.[12]

> Wilson: 'Am I to understand that if the whole civilized world asks Australia to agree to a mandate for these islands, Australia is prepared to defy the opinion of the whole civilized world?' Hughes: 'That's about the size of it Mr President.'
> WOODROW WILSON TO BILLY HUGHES

The discussion then descended further into farce when Lloyd George, trying to defuse the situation, asked whether Hughes would allow missionaries free access to New Guinea. Quick as a flash, he quipped, *Of course, I understand that these poor people are very short of food, and for some time past they have not have had enough missionaries.*[13] Wilson, for one, was not amused, though many others in the room doubtless were.

What did Hughes really say to Woodrow Wilson? There are at least eight accounts of Hughes' celebrated clash with Wilson over the New Guinea Mandate. Hankey's minute, quoted in the United States official record of the Conference, has Wilson asking 'if they were to understand that Australia and New Zealand were presenting an ultimatum' in favour of annexation or the 'C' class Mandate; and Hughes, replying after the question was repeated, that Wilson *had put it fairly well*. G Auchinloss, secretary to Colonel House, has Wilson saying that 'Australia and New Zealand with 6,000,000 people between them could not hold up a conference in which, including China, some 1,200 million people were represented.' Hughes's quips in reply about his representing *60,000 war dead* and about the natives eating missionaries appear to have originated in Hughes's own retelling of the story after the event, which is not necessarily to say that he had not actually made them.[14]

This rhetorical joust concluded, South Africa's Prime Minister General Louis Botha made a statesmanlike speech, the *status quo ante* was restored and the 'C' class Mandates formula was put forward and adopted.[15] Privately, however, Wilson fulminated that Hughes was a 'pestiferous varmint'.[16]

Given that the 'C' class Mandates were the agreed position of the British Empire delegation and that Hughes was *soi disant* a loyal member of it, Hughes' riling of Wilson suggests more than a characteristic display of mischief. It was a classic piece of ambit claim negotiating technique, whereby the negotiator, as in a wages dispute, asks for more than he expects to receive in the expectation of compromise later on. Hughes' extreme behaviour, as with Wilson's weaker histrionic attempt, was a ploy to remind the other side that the compromise position being put forward by more reasonable heads was preferable to a deadlock brought about by the adopting of inflexible, doctrinaire positions. If so, it worked a treat.

Next, the Mandates needed to be finally allocated to the

respective Mandatories under the various classes. Chaffing at the delay, Hughes wrote to House, on 5 May: *if peace were signed leaving Australia's position as regards the islands uncertain, there would be not only disappointment, but grave misgivings … that both the territorial integrity of their country and the White Australia policy, which is the corner stone of the national edifice, were in serious danger.*[17] In the absence of a constituted League of Nations, the Draft Covenant had been finally approved on 28 April in a plenary session. However, it was the Council of Ten, acting as the Supreme Council of the Allied and Associated Powers, to which, legally speaking, Germany had surrendered, which finally granted Mandates on 7 May; though, even then, these would have to be finally ratified by the League in due course.[18]

There were no surprises: Pacific Mandates went to Australia for New Guinea, New Zealand for Samoa and Japan for the Marshall and Caroline Islands. The detailed drawing up of the Mandate agreements was left to a Commission chaired by Lord Milner in June and July. Viscount Chinda, the Japanese member, tried to hold out for freedom of entry into and right to residence in the 'C' class Mandates. It was only when this claim was eventually withdrawn that the League finalised matters on 17 December 1920.[19]

As Hughes saw it, Japan was mounting a two-pronged assault on the White Australia policy. The other prong was Japan's campaign to have a racial equality clause inserted in the League of Nations Covenant. Such a clause, however benign, in Hughes' view might have been used to put up a legal challenge to Australia's restrictive immigration laws, initially as they applied in the Mandate and perhaps ultimately in Australia itself. The Japanese first proposed a draft clause to House and Wilson on 4 February, and this was massaged into what appeared to be an innocuous affirmation of the 'all men are created equal' variety, leaving individual countries to determine their actual immigration policies.

The United States and Canada, countries which had racially restrictive immigration policies similar to Australia's, were prepared to accept this pretence. In British Empire delegation meetings, however, Hughes and Massey (and Smuts *sotto voce*) were opposed to the clause in any form. The matter was first rejected by the British chairman Lord Robert Cecil, with the Dominions' pressure behind him, in the Commission on the League on 13 February. It came to a head, nevertheless, in a Council meeting on 11 April, when the Japanese again moved to have a racial equality clause inserted in the draft preamble to the League Covenant. Eleven of the 16 present voted for the clause, whereupon, inexplicably, Wilson ruled from the chair that, as the vote was not unanimous, it was not carried. In ensuing weeks, the Japanese, while still protesting in private, dropped their campaign. Wilson, for his part, blamed Hughes for torpedoing it. The truth is more complex and justifies Hughes' description of Wilson over the matter as *Mr Facing-both-ways*.[20]

There were a number of contexts and issues bearing on the debate. First was the United States' domestic position. The American West Coast was uniformly opposed to the Japanese clause and Wilson's support for it would tell against his Democratic Party there in the forthcoming Congressional elections. Furthermore, Wilson needed the votes of the West Coast Democrats to have his precious League of Nations ratified by Congress. Also, again for domestic reasons, Wilson had overtly excluded the Monroe Doctrine from the application of the League Covenant, much to the ire of the French. Circumstances were altering cases.

Hughes also had pressure on him domestically. For him it came from the Labor Party, which saw his 'failure' to annex New Guinea as a sign of his diluting the White Australia policy and feared worse was to come. Japanese domestic opinion was equally agitated in the other direction. The Japanese government, however, was prepared to broker a deal whereby in return for recognition of their rights in China and the north Pacific (the Okuma-Ishii Doctrine which paralleled the Monroe Doctrine), they would agree not to press the racial equality issue further. South Africa, Canada and New Zealand also had concerns about the implications for their racially discriminatory immigration and other policies.[21]

Major Frederic Eggleston of the Australian Delegation was out of sympathy with Hughes' machinations and a closet Wilsonian. He wrote in his diary for 15 February: 'Hughes delights in battle and takes the keenest delight in the kicks ... by which he gets things through. Of course he has the lust for power ... egotism ... quite overcome[s] his scruples ... I feel ... as if I had been living with dirty people ... Idealist is a term of abuse and there is nothing in the world like price and selfishness ... I have written some very learned memoranda ... but nobody ever reads them. To get Hughes to read anything you have to write in the style of a shilling shocker ... the fact is that Hughes has made up his mind about everything and does not want advice.'[22]

In his notes on one of the proposed amendments Hughes remarked in his inimitable way: *The Japanese want to insert the proposed amendment into the Preamble. It may be all right. But sooner than agree to it I would rather walk into the Seine – or the Folies Bergères [–] with my clothes off.*[23] In other words, it would be domestic political suicide. As, indeed, it would have been for Wilson.

Hughes, sensing that Wilson was wobbling in the direction of the Japanese, gave a widely reported interview to the Associated Press of America, intimating that the clause would be opposed root-and-branch in Australia as it would be on the

American West Coast. Next day Wilson was inundated with indignant cables from that very region.[24] House confided to the Japanese delegate, Baron Makino, that 'unless Hughes promised not to make trouble' the Americans could not support the clause. This time, then, Hughes was Wilson's willing catspaw.

Hughes said as much in an interview with the Japanese *Asahi* newspaper after the vote. There was a nation he would not name that *opposed the Japanese amendment ... and yet[,] pretended to be a nation friendly to Japan, and hiding behind Australia, wanted to have it falsely said that the responsibility for the rejection of the race equality claim rested on Australia alone.* The Japanese people were not *fools* but were *shrewd and intelligent* and could see through that ruse.[25]

Careful American diplomacy sealed the deal. Japan was delighted to get Mandates for Shandong and the islands north of the Equator. Meanwhile, Wilson quietly had a clause inserted in the League Covenant guaranteeing that all votes on changing it had to be unanimous. This not only retrospectively justified his actions over the vote in Council on the racial equality clause, it also satisfied Hughes. As long as there was an Australian delegate at League of Nations meetings the White Australia policy would be safe.[26]

Hughes reported to Watt after the newspaper interview: *Japanese here ... greatly prefer straight-out opponent to those who promised support ... Makino ... knows that if Wilson had had courage to vote for them, or to accept two to one majority vote, their amendment would have been inserted. Do not worry.*[27] Harold Nicolson, one of the British officials, noted in his diary quite astutely and correctly, that Hughes 'rescued the President by the skin of his teeth'.[28] How right he was. House noted with some satisfaction in his private diary that the Americans were delighted to have shifted the blame for opposing the racial equality clause to the British: 'It has taken considerable finesse to lift the load from our shoulders and place it upon the British, but it has been done.'[29]

Hughes again was a scapegoat for the Great Powers and for some of the British Empire delegation; but the short-term opprobrium of the right-thinking liberal internationalists was something Hughes was happy to bear provided he gained the substance of his policies, as he did in this case and in relation to New Guinea. On issues where he did not have Imperial support he would fare less well.

7

Dividing the Spoils, 1919

Control of New Guinea was mainly about defence, and opposing the racial equality clause was about immigration and White Australia. The other two important issues – reparations and indemnities, and the mandate for Nauru – were about finance and trade (though commerce was also a factor with New Guinea). Hughes had pinned his colours to the mast on reparations as early as 1916 as a 'Germany must pay' man, and he continued in this vein. Nauru was vital to key sectors of the Australian economy: wheat, wool and meat.

The reparations issue was referred to a Commission under the chairmanship of L L Klotz, the French Finance Minister. Hughes, one of its three British members, was elected one of two deputy chairmen and became chairman of one of its three sub-committees, that looking into methods of payment. The first meeting of the full Commission was on 3 February and on the 10th it fell to Hughes to lead for the British delegation. He argued for full repayment of war costs on three main grounds.

The first was legal principle: *The Principle of justice upon which the right of reparation is founded is that, when a wrong has been done and suffered, the wrong-doer, should, to the full extent of his capacity, right the wrong. It is a matter of compensation, not of punishment. It is based on the idea that, so far as possible, the burden of the wrong done should fall on the wrong-doer, not on the innocent victim.*

Second, he argued that restoration and compensation were one and the same: *Australia has lost nearly 60,000 men killed and many more maimed for life. She has incurred a war debt of £300,000,000 – a crushing burden for 5,000,000 people. And what is true of Australia, is true mutatis mutandis, of the other Dominions and peoples of the British Empire. In the way of destruction of civilian life and property they may have suffered little. Yet the sacrifice they have made, and damage they have suffered, have not been less. There must be for them, as for all the Allies, full compensation.*

'Aggressive war is a crime against which the nations of the world must inflexibly set their faces, to threaten with dire penalties those nations who in the future may dare to disturb the world's peace ...'

BILLY HUGHES, 10 FEBRUARY 1919

Last came the issue of punishment: *Aggressive war is a crime against which the nations of the world must inflexibly set their faces, to threaten with dire penalties those nations who in the future may dare to disturb the world's peace ... Germany deliberately plunged the world into dreadful war. She has inflicted upon its peoples horrors and almost incalculable damage. She must purge herself of her iniquity and atone for her crime. So far as is humanly possible she must repair the damage she has caused and put the allied nations back where they stood in 1914.*[1] This was a powerful piece of advocacy such as a criminal prosecutor would make before a jury and no doubt it impressed the Commission.

Three days later, at the next meeting, John Foster Dulles, only 30 years old and a rising corporate lawyer, replied drily and concisely for the United States. The Americans agreed about Germany's guilt, he said, but the fact was that the terms of the Armistice constituted a contract between Germany and the Allied and Associated Powers; and that contract only mentioned restoration of direct damage done as a result of the War, not payment of war costs. Only Belgium, whose invasion was a direct violation of an international agreement, deserved full cost compensation. Lord Sumner, for the British, then put forward a number of precedents – 1815 when Napoleon's France had to pay a hefty indemnity to the allies, and 1871 when France had to pay Germany – to which Dulles coolly replied that each contract was different and precedent, therefore, was irrelevant.

Next day, having burnt the midnight oil with his legal advisers, Garran and Latham, Hughes took on Dulles on his own terms. If Belgium deserved full compensation, then those who had aided Belgium, notably the British Empire and France, deserved it too. If this did not apply then the collective security principle proposed for the new League of Nations was a *travesty*. He later underlined this point in a written rejoinder to Dulles which said that no nation would enter a League of Nations-sponsored war if they were likely to bankrupt themselves in the process. Dulles replied on 19 February saying that the Belgium argument benefited only some of the Allies, but ignored those who had not entered the War as a direct result of the invasion of Belgium. He, therefore, recommended that the matter be referred to the Supreme War Council for guidance, and this advice was accepted.[2]

Some unofficial recollections of proceedings suggest a more mordant flavour to Hughes's participation. Thomas

Lamont, one of the American advisers, recalled Hughes 'turning around and shaking his finger at the American delegation' before he shouted, *Some people in this war have not been so near the fire as we British have, and, therefore, being unburned, they have a cold, detached view of the situation.* On another occasion he referred to Dr Wilhelm Solf, the German Foreign Minister, as having hoodwinked Wilson, by crawling through his peace notes *like a serpent through dead leaves.*[3]

It is no surprise, then, that the reparations issue quickly descended into deadlock. At this point, however, Dulles came up with two very effective stratagems. The first was the proposed insertion of a War Guilt clause into the Peace Treaty. If Germany admitted moral responsibility for the War then financial payment would become a secondary, practical issue. The second was to say that any call for full war costs would lessen the amounts going to France and Belgium, the so-called 'play of percentages'. These ingenious ploys had the effect of splitting the Allied camp. Add to this Lloyd George's concerns that a crippled German economy would be a menace to British prosperity and that eventually Britain's £6 billion war debt to the United States would itself need to be confronted, and it is no wonder that the Americans had the whip hand.

Hughes cast around for allies. But this time the other big Dominions were not with him. Canada had made money out of the War and South Africa had not paid much and stood to gain mineral-rich South-West Africa. Citing the generous terms which had ended the Anglo-South African War at the Treaty of Vereeniging in 1902, Smuts and Botha recommended compromise. Further, Smuts got the Americans to agree to the inclusion of war pensions in the equation, thus giving a sop to the British Empire countries. Horse-trading among the Council of Four eventually led to agreement to divide the reparations on a ratio of 3:2:1 to France, the British Empire and Belgium respectively.[4]

Hughes was bitterly disappointed. In a minority of one in the British Empire delegation, he wrote to Lloyd George in capitulation: *You and your colleagues of the British Government, and all Dominion Prime Ministers except myself, have approved the proposal for Reparation which you laid before us. You have assured us that you cannot get better terms. I much regret it, and hope even now that some way may be found of securing agreement for demanding Reparation commensurate with the tremendous sacrifices made by the British Empire and her Allies. But if this be indeed impossible, and the proposal as it stands is inserted in the Treaty of Peace, I shall sign it.*[5]

Lloyd George's reply was frank and withering: 'I quite understand your attitude. It is a very well known one. It is generally called "heads I win, and tails you lose" which means that you get the full benefit from the arrangement we have painfully elaborated in compensation and especially in pensions, whereas your comrades in the Dominions, in Great Britain and in France get all the abuse.'[6]

The fixing of the amount to be divided up was placed in the hands of a standing Commission to report in two years' time, thus effectively side-lining any further work by the Reparations Commission, including Hughes's sub-committee, which had not come to any conclusions. Hughes reported the expected general outcome to his government on 4 May: *Reparation is fixed at about 11,000,000,000 [pounds], of which 1,000,000,000 pounds, more or less, are to be paid within just two years. The balance is to be spread over a term of years and a Commission is to take charge ... Out of [the]* total amount France gets 55%, say 7,000,000,000 pounds, the British Empire gets somewhere about 2,000,000,000 pounds, or about one fifth of the whole. Australia's share of this will be (as cost of war is not included) about one twenty-fifth [£80m] ... spread over twenty, fifty or a million years, more or less ... Belgium is much better treated than we are ... [though] her war debt is much less than ours. She lost in war only about one-half as many men as we did. Her casualties were less than a half. France has suffered terribly and I grudge her nothing.[7]

He was even more candid in a letter to Munro Ferguson: All the indemnity we get will hardly pay for repatriation let alone the cost of war and pensions. At least I fear so. It is not a good Peace for Australia, nor indeed for Britain. It is a good Peace for America. She who did not come into the war to make anything has made thousands of millions out of it. She gets the best ships. She has a good chance of beating us for the world mercantile supremacy. She prevented us getting the cost of the war. Wilson's 14 points has [sic] been the millstone round our necks all through the Conference.[8]

> 'It is *not* a good Peace for Australia, nor indeed for Britain. It *is* a good Peace for America.'
> BILLY HUGHES, 17 MAY 1919

The war cost Australia some £464 million, of which £100 million was initially claimed as reparations. In the event, the apportioning of the British Empire share in 1921 projected a payment over many years of just £50 million. By 1931, when payments ceased altogether, Australia had received only £5,571,720. This came mostly in kind in the form of German ships confiscated in Australian ports and German property confiscated in New Guinea.[9]

If New Guinea proved to be a spoil of war in the economic

sense, with its copra plantations and potential for mineral discoveries, of much more immediate economic importance was the former German island of Nauru. This tiny speck in the Pacific to the east of New Guinea, only some 2,271 hectares in size, had 1,806 hectares, or some 300 million tons, of phosphate (representing millennia of bird droppings or guano). This was a century's supply of invaluable agricultural fertiliser right on the Australian farmer's doorstep. At the time it was meeting 80 per cent of Australia's phosphate requirements. In the absence of significant reparations, such an asset was well worth fighting for.[10]

Before the War a British firm, the Pacific Phosphate Company chaired by Lord Balfour of Burleigh, had worked the island's deposits under a lease from the German government. They also mined the guano on nearby Ocean Island, which was a British colony. In 1914 the British were expelled by the German officials, but they were soon re-instated when the island came under Australian military occupation following the German capitulation at Rabaul in September. For administrative convenience during the War the island fell within the civil jurisdiction of the British Deputy Commissioner for the Western Pacific, though he was answerable in military matters to the Australian government. After the War, however, the Australians thought Nauru should be under the Australian Administrator at Rabaul.

Matters came to a head when the Pacific Phosphate Company applied to resume its pre-war arrangements, asked for the Australian garrison to be removed and claimed it had 82 years of its lease left to run. The Australian government replied asking to see the written agreement and the company refused to supply it, either because it did not have it or because it was with the superseded German authority and legally dubious. Hughes asked that Nauru should be an Australian Mandate. Milner, now at the Colonial Office, argued that its proximity to Ocean Island suggested it should be British. Massey, for New Zealand, also expressed an interest.[11]

As was his wont, Hughes pulled out all stops to get Nauru. In a letter to Milner the day before the Council of Four met to decide its fate, Hughes stated: *Australia, alone of the Dominions, in addition to the heavy cost in life, and money, of the war effort, has had to face the disastrous fact that she could not get her products to market. Whilst other Dominions were growing rich on the sale of their produce at war prices, Australia having stripped herself of shipping for the sake of the urgent transport needs of the Empire, was unable to market the bulk of her produce at all; and has suffered more than other parts of the Empire. This is a fact which should certainly be taken into consideration. The matter is one of fundamental importance and the non-recognition of Australia's claim ... would have the most unfortunate effect in every way.*[12] Special pleading aside – New Zealand was in the same boat and much of the Australian product was pre-sold – it was evident that Hughes was prepared for a showdown.

In the upshot, however, the matter was dealt with by means of a neat diplomatic compromise. The Council of Four decided that the Mandate should go to 'His Britannic Majesty', effectively leaving it up to the British Empire to sort out how Australian, British and New Zealand interests should be reconciled. Hughes had been prepared not to sign the Treaty had he not got control of Nauru for Australia, but his Cabinet at home refused to back him. He was forced *to make best of a bad job.*[13] Nevertheless, he got much of what he wanted.

The Nauru Mandate was to be executed by a commission

of three, with one member each from Australia, Britain and New Zealand, who would take turns to administer the island. No one, not even Wilson, thought to consult the islanders themselves about their future. The Pacific Phosphate Company was bought out by the three governments for £3.5 million, with the Australian and British governments each paying 42 per cent and New Zealand 16 per cent. The phosphate sales were divided in the same proportions.[14] Had Hughes not fought Australia's corner, the Pacific Phosphates Company would have got its way and Britain the sole Mandate. As it was, Hughes had secured a direct 42 per cent stake and a say for Australia in the future. At 1919 prices Australia's share of the phosphate would amount to some £168 million over the next half-century.[15] Australia's wheat farmers and pastoralists had good cause to be grateful to him.

On the broad question of the League of Nations, Hughes remained an *undisguised sceptic*.[16] For him, the proof of the pudding would be in the eating. He outlined his position in some memorable interventions at the Imperial War Council. On 26 November 1918, the minutes record: ... *he objected to President Wilson's views, which he interpreted as meaning a world-State and the surrender by the Great Powers of their self-governing rights. No country would allow its vital interests to be decided by anyone else except itself. Mr. Hughes then gave various concrete cases to explain his meaning. One of these was that in Australia we had a continent that would hold 100,000,000 people, whereas the Australian population only amounted to 5,000,000. We were going to say to thousands of millions of people that no one else should come to Australia – which we had no moral right to do. If the question went to a League of Nations the Australian view would not be supported. Mr. Hughes eventually suggested that the best solution would be an agreement between the United States and Great Britain, which would ensure the peace of the world.*[17]

Free trade and disarmament were other cases in point. Again, he said on 30 December 1918: *It was intolerable ... for President Wilson to dictate to us how the world was to be governed. If the saving of civilisation had depended on the United States, it would have been in tears and chains today. As regards the League of Nations, Mr. Hughes considered that a League of Nations which was to endure and weather the storms of time would have to be a thing like the British Empire, framed in accordance with historical associations and practical needs. President Wilson, however, had no practical scheme at all, and no proposals would bear the test of experience ...*

He went on to explain his position further: *Speaking for Australia, he wanted to know what Australia was to get for the sacrifices she had made. When he had secured what he wanted, the Freedom of the Seas, as we knew it and meant to have it [Australia supported Britain fully over the right to blockade], and necessary guarantees for the security and development of the Empire and reparation and indemnities, then he would have no objection to handing over other matters to a League of Nations. Such a League must, however, be properly constituted, and one in which the British Empire occupied a place corresponding to its sacrifices in the war and its position in the world. He insisted that in any case we should not commit ourselves to the League ... until the Conference had completed its labours. To start with the League of Nations and continually refer everything to this League would mean giving up the substance for the shadow. The League of Nations should be the gilded ball on the dome of the cathedral and not the foundation-stone.*[18] As it was, as we have seen, the Covenant and the other elements of the Treaty proceeded more or less along parallel tracks.

Hughes played no direct part on the Commission on the League of Nations, but he did write a memorandum objecting to some of the terms of the Draft Covenant. He objected to the use of the term 'executive' to describe the League Council, as its job was to advise and make recommendations to the sovereign states who were its members not to legislate for them. Similarly, sanctions and declarations of war were to be recommended – not made mandatory. The League was an instrument for 'international co-operation' not a 'supranational government'. He was unsuccessful in his opposition to mandatory sanctions (though history would prove him mostly correct *de facto*), but he did gain his other points, and the covenant was altered. Clearly, he spoke for a significant number of delegates.[19]

Hughes did sign the Peace Treaty on 28 June 1919, but his position on the League remained unchanged. As he had told the diners at a British Empire League Luncheon at Claridge's Hotel in London the week before: *I welcome the League of Nations ... But does anyone think the League will bottle up human nature? Australia is the most distant outpost of white civilisation. The real problem is – if we are attacked, shall we call upon the British Empire or the League of Nations for help? What will Australia's position be in times of trouble if the British Navy is part of a polyglot, heterogeneous force attached to the League, which probably will contain our deadly enemy? ... If the navy is controlled by others, or whittled down, there will be the beginning of the end of the Empire.*[20] Hughes never viewed the League of Nations other than as an experiment and he never failed to make the point that the Empire should keep its powder dry.

Nevertheless, the international position of the Dominions was enhanced as a consequence of the peacemaking process. The blood and treasure sacrifice of the War won them seats at the Conference table. Each joined the new League of Nations in its own right, though the signing of the Treaty document itself reflected a more anomalous position. For Britain and the British Empire their 'High Contracting Party' was their collective monarch and head of state, King George V. So, when it came to signing, the British Empire signed as one. First came the signatures of the five British Cabinet Ministers. These were followed by the indented names

> I welcome the League of Nations ... But does anyone think the League will bottle up human nature?
>
> **BILLY HUGHES, 23 JUNE 1919**

of the Dominions with the signatures of their representatives beside them. Thus the Dominions, though notionally independent and equal, were still legally all part of a greater sovereign entity. How this worked out in practice would be another matter.

Hughes was, however, content with this arrangement. Ever the realist, he observed: *The Dominions as part of the Empire are listened to by foreign nations with interest, for the influence of a great world-Power lends weight to their lightest word ... In themselves, although potentially great nations ... they do not count for much; as part of an Empire that ... has behind it great riches and organised force, the world pays them the tribute it always gives to wealth and power.*[21] Empire mattered.

Caught short without an official seal to affix to the Treaty, Hughes and Garran scoured the antique and bric-à-brac shops and stalls of Paris. The selection narrowed to a choice between Hercules slaying a dragon and the three-legged device of the Isle of Man. We shall never know whether it was out of modesty or Celtic pride that Hughes chose the three legs.[22]

When the ex-German transport *Friedrichsruh* docked at Fremantle on 23 August 1919, it bore 1,200 returning soldiers and Australia's Prime Minister. It was a triumphant return. Making speeches all the way, and mobbed at each stop by crowds of his beloved Diggers and civilian well-wishers, Billy Hughes proceeded by train for a week via Adelaide to Melbourne. As the *Argus* reported of his arrival in Melbourne: 'Looking down Collins Street[,] one saw a huge swaying mass of men and women. There were no barricades, no well-ordered ranks marching in procession, no formidable force of troopers to cleave a way through the crowd. Only a single motor car with a little man perched on high, supported by a dozen enthusiastic "diggers", and waving his hand to the mighty crowd that surged around him. And what a crowd! It swept up Collins Street like a great tide; it filled the whole width from doorway to doorway. And all the time it cheered itself hoarse for the sake of the little man in the motor car. It was a great tribute to a man who had done great things.'[23]

In this heady atmosphere, on 10 September he addressed Parliament on the subject of the Peace Treaty and the need for it to be accepted.[24] It was a statesmanlike speech, characteristically pungent and proud by degrees. He made no bones about his opposition to basing the Treaty on the Fourteen Points: *that was an error – of judgement if you like – for by these fourteen points adopted as the basis of Peace, none of those things for which Australia had fought was guaranteed.* But each of the Dominions demanded, and eventually received, separate representation, which was their due. The Treaty was *as large as the Pickwick Papers*. It contained strictures to curb future German aggression, such as reducing the armed forces and fleet, demilitarising the Rhineland, and returning Alsace-Lorraine and other territories.

He was cautiously optimistic about another 'guarantee', the League of Nations: *The League of Nations does not attempt to govern the world. It attempts, rather, to set up the machinery by which civilized men, if they will act as Christianity and common sense dictate, may avoid war. It lights the way to a better road. It does not make that road, nor does it carry us along it. We must walk. But if the whole of the nations of the world are really desirous to co-operate in this great work, then the League of Nations is truly a charter of Liberty – a charter of civilization – of no less value to the world than was Magna Carta to the men of our race; no less great than the setting up of the role [sic] of law for the rule of force among our own ancestors in the old days of tribal struggle and barbaric strife.* He was careful to say that the Monroe Doctrine was exempted from the League and that Australia desired to set up a similar regional doctrine *relating to our sphere in the Pacific.*[25]

Moving on to Australia's specific position, he asked, *Now, what have we got?* First, *national safety* was ensured when it was agreed *the great rampart of islands stretching around the north-east of Australia should be held by us.* Second, the White Australia policy was guaranteed. He explained the position carefully, using a homely analogy: *Because I do not invite every man in this Parliament into my house, it cannot be said that I do not regard him as an equal … We claim the right … to say in regard to Australia who shall enter and who shall not. This is our house. To keep it ours, our soldiers have sacrificed their blood, and they have placed the keys in our hands. The war was waged for liberty. We had this right before, and we claim to retain it now.*

Third, on reparations, he believed that *the German people have committed an offence, nay, a crime, the most bloody and desperate the world has ever known, and they must pay the penalty*. But the British and Americans thought differently. Australia's war cost £464 million, but Australia would be lucky to receive £100 million in due course and only £5 to 8 million by 1921. He went on: *If this peace be unjust, it is not unjust to Germany. It is very unjust to those free people who had to fight a battle of life and death for their very existence ... To ask us to pay, and call that justice, would be an abuse of the word. This Peace, whatever may be said, is not a harsh Peace to Germany, and it is not a just Peace to us.*[26]

'This Peace, whatever may be said, is not a harsh Peace to Germany, and it is not a just Peace to us.'
BILLY HUGHES, 10 SEPTEMBER 1919

And he finished with a eulogy to the Anzacs: *If the fruits of victory are to be measured by national safety and liberty, and the high ideals for which these boys died, the sacrifice has not been in vain. They died for the safety of Australia. Australia is safe. They died for liberty, and liberty is now assured to us and to all men. They have made for themselves and their country a name that will not die.*[27] Needless to say, later in September both Houses of Parliament voted to approve the Treaty.

In this speech were the seeds of a potent national myth. Battling Billy Hughes had stood up to the world, represented the Anzacs' blood sacrifice and guaranteed Australia's liberty, safety and way of life against all comers. What he did not say, was that he stood on the shoulders of the other Dominions and Britain (and occasionally France, Italy and even Japan and the United States) to do so. His success over the Pacific Islands Mandate owed much to the backing of the British

Empire, France, Italy and Japan. He needed Dominion and United States backing to defeat the racial equality clause and guarantee White Australia. Without British and American backing he failed dismally over reparations. He did, however, manage some compensation on the side by brokering a three-way deal within the British Empire delegation (with Britain and New Zealand) to secure at a bargain price a long-term supply of phosphates for his farmers and graziers. Using his British world connections, and all his political skills, Hughes had scrambled his way to a qualified but mainly successful outcome.

William Hughes and the Prime Minister of New Zealand William Massey
outside 10 Downing Street in 1921.

III
The Legacy

8

On Top of the British World? 1919–23

The next four years were a paradoxical period for Hughes. Internationally, as a leading figure in the British world, his influence and reputation were at their zenith. He was at his most effective at the Imperial Conference of 1921, which laid the foundations for more than a decade of accord in the Pacific. Domestically, while he had some policy successes, his long absence from the political scene had put him out of touch with his electoral base. The tide which would eventually sweep him from office soon turned inexorably against him.

A dominant factor in the international position immediately after the Peace Conference was the unresolved matter of arms control. Germany and its allies had been muzzled, but when the United States failed to join the new League of Nations, *ad hoc* arrangements became the order of the day. The naval balance was what concerned strategists most. A naval race had developed between the United States and Japan, the Royal Navy was in danger of lagging behind especially in the Pacific and the Anglo-Japanese Treaty was up for renewal. This was the immediate context to the Imperial War Conference which met in London from June to August 1921.

Hughes' opening speech at the Conference was a *tour de force*.[1] He began by praising the idea that the Imperial War Cabinet was being continued in peace time. *[W]e are resolved to continue along that path in company, being guided by each other's counsel and believing firmly that in co-operation and in unity lies the safety of all, and, in no small degree, the peace and welfare of the world*. He said he hoped they would

'... in co-operation and in unity lies the safety of all, and, in no small degree, the peace and welfare of the world.'

BILLY HUGHES, 7 APRIL 1921

find *a practical and sure way of bridging that apparently impossible chasm which divides complete autonomy of the several parts of the Empire from united action upon matters affecting us all*. This was *essential if this Conference is not to be a last magnificent flare of a dying illumination*. He then went on to the key issues: the Anglo-Japanese Treaty, naval defence and *improved communication*.

On the Anglo-Japanese Treaty, he had claimed in a Parliamentary speech just before he left Australia that it was *a thing more precious than rubies that we should have an alliance with the greatest Power in the East*.[2] Needless to say, he reported that Australia was in favour of renewal. However, Australians also had *a very warm corner in their hearts for America*; so, to allay American suspicions, any treaty had to exclude explicitly any war with the United States. It also had to conform to the League of Nations Covenant. On the other hand, Japan should not be left *isolated*. Therefore, a United States-Japan conference should precede treaty renewal.

Related to this was disarmament. America might be suspicious of the United Kingdom, but the Dominions were *replicas of themselves* free from *Imperialistic ambitions*. Noting that *the appalling race for naval superiority has already begun … [and] This vicious rivalry grows on what it feeds on*, he suggested that a *lead* should be given for talks between the United States, Japan, France and Britain. *If the world resolves to stop making preparations for war, everything is possible.* Nevertheless, the Empire *must have such naval defence as is adequate for our safety* and this would be *cheaper and better with disarmament*, provided *relative strengths* were maintained. It was a *corollary of admission into the councils of Empire* that a financial contribution should be made by each member. And, on defence, he concluded: *The ambitions of men and nations are curbed by their material power. In our case sea power is, and must always be, the determining factor of our policy … The Dominions would not exist if it were not for the British Navy … We are a united Empire or we are nothing.*

On the idea of an Imperial constitution or Imperial federation, however, Hughes said they should *leave well alone*. The Dominions were totally free to make treaties and have embassies and some did so – the Canadians had opened an embassy in Washington. Improved cooperation and communication by telephone, radio, air and fast ships was the answer. If this connected and networked British world had proved itself in wartime, the opportunity was there to prove itself even more in the years of peace.

In subsequent meetings, Hughes crossed swords with the Canadians, South Africans and British on how this vision might be realised. Arthur Meighen, the Canadian Prime Minister, wanted to tread softly with the United States and not renew the Anglo-Japanese Treaty until after multi-lateral disarmament talks. Hughes opposed him. The United States had rejected the League and *we are in it*, he said. Japan was a great naval power with whom Australia and the Empire had to treat: *I, for one, will vote against any renewal ... upon one condition and one only, and that is that America gives us the assurance of safety which our circumstances demand.* Meighen spoke, he said, from the geopolitical safety of North America – *he has at his door a powerful neighbour who for its own sake, if not his, will defend him.* Meighen was making the case for isolationist America whereas he, Hughes, who represented a vulnerable, under-populated Australia with 13,000 miles of coastline facing a proximate Asia with a *thousand millions* of people needing space, took a different view. In the end, the United States relieved the situation by inviting Britain to a conference to discuss the Pacific and disarmament, and it was decided that treaty renewal could be deferred until after the conference.[3]

The naval situation was critical, especially in the light of the 'Geddes axe' spending cuts in Britain immediately after the War. It emerged in discussion that the Royal Navy had 29 battleships with none being built, the United States 36 with 11 being built and Japan 9 with 8 being built. Since the United States and British were two- (or even three- or four-) ocean navies and the Japanese a one-ocean navy, the Japanese were verging on becoming the most powerful navy in the Pacific. The United States Navy already had global superiority.[4] It was proposed, and Hughes and Massey strongly supported the idea, that the expansion of the Royal Navy should be the first call on German reparations (estimated in 1921 at £33 to 44 million for the British Empire as a whole) when they came, and that parity with the United States Navy should be the aim. Eight capital ships would cost £60 million. Each part of the Empire would pay according to its economic capacity: Britain 86.75 per cent, Canada 4.35 per cent, Australia 4.35 per cent, New Zealand 1.75 per cent, South Africa 0.60 per cent, India 1.20 per cent and so on. Hughes pronounced that Australia would pay, but when Smuts and Meighen refused, the plan faltered. It was agreed to wait and see what happened at the projected Washington Naval Conference scheduled for the end of the year.[5] In the meantime, a major naval base should be built in Singapore to support any Far Eastern Fleet which might be assembled against a Japanese threat.

Smuts's plan for a federal Imperial constitution was buried by Meighen and Hughes. Hughes put it caustically in a letter to Cook, who was Acting Prime Minister: *The constitutional tinkers are securely soldered up in their own can.*[6] But Hughes, nevertheless, was much in favour of improved Imperial communications. As he put it at the Conference when speaking of *this wide-flung Empire – a world within a world: … [W]ireless communication, faster steamships communication, airships – all those things have relation to the same problem; they tend to bind the different parts of the Empire closer together. They make it a more profitable thing for every citizen in every part of the Empire to be a citizen of this Empire. We should not forget or cease to advocate that it is not only a very glorious thing to be a citizen of this Empire, but it is a very profitable thing as it is now, and it can be made still more profitable.*[7]

Like many of his political generation across the British world, he pursued the economic and emotional unity of the Empire while at the same time rejecting central political control in favour of a happy and pragmatic collaboration among democratic equals. He mused further on this wider point a week or so later: *When I stand up in the Parliament of the Commonwealth of Australia, even though my feet rest upon a British statute as a legal foothold, I cannot see how I could be clothed with greater amplitude of authority if we were independent nations ... [W]hat should we be outside this Empire? Our voice would be lost across the waste of waters, the voice of a community of five and a half millions of people. But when we speak as part of the Empire, on behalf of the Empire, the voice of Australia is heard.*[8] Airships, radio and faster steamers would help cement new links.

At the 1921 Imperial Conference, Hughes argued for an airship service, in which flights from Britain to Australia would take about ten days. In the detailed discussion, Hughes was opposed by Winston Churchill, British Secretary of State for the Colonies. It emerged that airships cost £320,000 each, and three or four would be required; and that aeroplanes cost £10,000 each, but they had much smaller carrying capacity. Masts to dock the airships would cost £300,000 each, and five or six would be required. In all, the scheme would cost some £3 million to set up and £500,000 per annum to operate. It was suggested that Britain would foot half the bill, and Australia, India, New Zealand and South Africa would pay equal shares of the other half.

In 1919 Hughes' government had sponsored an air race to Australia from London for a prize of £10,000. It was won by two members of the Australian Flying Corps, Ross and Keith Smith, in an adapted Vickers Vimy bomber. The flight took them just under 28 days in November and December.[9] This was a week shorter than the five-week sea journey and it proved that a regular service was possible.

In the wash-up, despite Hughes's strong advocacy and his insistence on its eventual commercial viability, the decision fell to Churchill, who set aside the full vision as too expensive. Hughes continued to press the issue for some time afterwards, but the wreck of the *R34* airship with the loss of 44 lives later in the year put a final stop to the plan. Commercial flight between Australia and Britain would take another decade to materialise, though regular mail flights started internally in

Australia in 1922 with government subsidies.[10] Similarly, an Australasian plan to instigate a special fast cruiser or yacht service across the Pacific to shorten travel time to London foundered on cost grounds.[11]

Regarding radio, Hughes argued that powerful transmitters along German and French lines should be built in Britain and each Dominion so that there could be direct communication between them. In this he was advised by Ernest Fisk, managing director of Amalgamated Wireless (Australasia) (AWA), a Marconi-trained English techni-cian and experimenter now based in Sydney. Churchill opposed this idea, too, suggesting instead the Norman Scheme, which con-

Billy Hughes and Cook had made the first wireless broadcast to Australia from Britain on 22 September 1919. It was received in Sydney by Ernest Fisk at AWA.

sisted of a chain of smaller relay transmitters stretched across the Empire at 2,000-mile intervals. Again, Hughes lost the fight on cost grounds. Australia opted out and, after the Conference, the Hughes government bought a controlling interest in AWA for £500,001 and Hughes sat on its board for the rest of his life. After some delay, AWA's inter-continental station was opened in 1927.[12]

The investment in AWA was along the lines of several other of Hughes' nation-building schemes, which today we would call public-private initiatives. Another, which pre-dated the Imperial Conference, was a deal in 1919 with the Anglo-Persian Oil Company to establish Commonwealth Oil Refineries (COR). The Australian government took just over half the shares in COR and Anglo-Persian the rest. The deal turned on Anglo-Persian's building a refinery in Australia and supplying cut-price oil in return for exploration rights in Papua. Before this, the only oil in Australia was provided by two American companies and one Dutch company. The

British government also had a controlling interest in the Anglo-Persian element so as to guarantee oil supplies to the Royal Navy. At this time, Hughes also tried and failed to establish a Vickers aircraft factory in Australia.[13] Further nation-building initiatives were the establishment of the Institute of Science and Industry, forerunner of the Commonwealth Scientific and Industrial Research Organisation, to carry out applied research, and the beginnings of a national highway plan and a national electricity grid. The transcontinental rail link to Perth had opened in 1917.

Hughes also worked out with Parliamentary Under-Secretary of State for the Colonies Amery the basis for the British Empire Settlement Act of 1922, under which Australia and Britain would share the costs of a great wave of assisted migration to Australia for the rest of the decade.[14] In asides at the Imperial Conference, he spoke against any concessions to Egyptian nationalism and Greek claims in Turkey, pronouncing that the Anzacs had found the Egyptians and Greeks corrupt and the Turks worthy of support.

Hughes soon found that domestic political circumstances forbade his participation in the Washington Conferences of November 1921 to February 1922, and he sent George Pearce in his stead. In a series of treaties, these Conferences, involving the United States, Japan, the British Empire (including Australia), France and Italy, confirmed the territorial *status quo* in the Pacific, guaranteed nations would consult before acting but not aid each other mandatorily, and set fleet sizes in a ratio of 5:5:3 for the British Empire, the United States and Japan. This meant fleet reductions for the British Empire and United States, and also that the United States and the British Empire, as multiple-ocean navies, would need to combine to counter Japan's one-ocean strength in the Pacific.

It was a qualified victory, but it established an uneasy peace in the Pacific for another ten years. As a result of the fleet reduction programme, the battle cruiser HMAS *Australia*, flagship of the RAN, was scuttled off Sydney Heads in 1924, three of Australia's six cruisers were moth-balled and naval expenditure reduced by a fifth. As Hughes put it in Parliament, Australia was now more than ever dependent on the strength of the Royal Navy.[15]

In small wars, however, Britain could not necessarily expect Australian participation. In 1920 Hughes had quietly refused an Australian battalion to combat an Imperial brush fire in Mesopotamia.[16] Then, in September 1922, Hughes learned from the press that Lloyd George, deserted militarily and diplomatically by the French and Italians, had committed Imperial troops once more to the Dardanelles. This was to support the small British occupation garrison in Chanak on the Asian coast of the Sea of Marmara against Turkish attempts to win back their territory lost in the Treaty of Sèvres (1920). The Greeks had already been driven from nearby Smyrna. Chanak was a delicate issue as it took in the Gallipoli Peninsula and, potentially, Australian war graves. In public, Hughes supported Lloyd George, saying Australia would if necessary send troops, but in private he sent an excoriating cable which vented all his worst fears.

Hughes resented not being consulted, though he himself had not consulted Cabinet or Parliament before committing troops. This, he wrote to Lloyd George, was *a bolt from the blue*. Where, he asked, was the diplomatic unity of the Empire? Australians were *sick of war* and would only fight to defend *vital national interests*. They would not help further the Imperial *ambitions* of that German sympathiser, King Constantine of Greece. The League of Nations should discuss the issue and a legal solution should be found before force was applied. In the event, the storm blew over. New Zealand and Newfoundland had offered Britain unqualified support, but Canada and South Africa had refused. The support was not needed; the military stand-off led to talks, and the League and Great Powers blessed the negotiated solution spelled out in the Treaty of Lausanne of 23 July 1923, which gave the Turks control of all of their former territory.

The Chanak fiasco was one of the factors in Lloyd George's fall in October 1922.[17] The League had fudged a test of strength. Plainly, force still mattered in international affairs and world opinion was variable and malleable. For realists like Hughes the question now resolved itself, yet again as ever, into whether Australia's vital interests and Britain's and the United States' would always tally.

After the 1921 Conference Hughes returned to a domestic political cyclone. He had not won his khaki election convincingly in December 1919, and only held office on the sufferance of the newly emerged Country Party, which represented farming and pastoral interests still chafing under wartime price controls. In the new lower house, elected for the first time under the preferential voting system, the Nationals had 37 members, the Country Party 11, and Labor 26, plus 1 independent National. Should the Country Party switch sides the government would struggle to stay in power.

When Hughes had left for the Imperial Conference of 1921 he had extracted an informal agreement from Earle Page, the Country Party leader, to support the government during his absence, but the truce ended soon after his return. The Country Party criticised Hughes' favouring of city manufacturing interests behind tariff walls and wished to have marketing control of primary products returned to the producers, which Hughes gradually conceded industry by industry. They called for general retrenchment, and Page coined the catch phrase 'Drop the Loot' to signify Hughes' supposed stealing from public funds to support pet projects. Watt, a dyed-in-the-wool, old-fashioned Liberal who never liked Hughes, resigned from the Treasurership while on a trip to London to renegotiate wool and wheat sales, citing undue interference from the Prime Minister. S M Bruce, who became Treasurer in December 1921, had criticised the Commonwealth Shipping Line for its post-war losses and called for its sale. And Latham, one of the advisers who had been privately

The Commonwealth Shipping Line cost Hughes £2,047,000 in 1916 and, under favourable wartime conditions, paid for itself within two years and made a profit of £1 million in 1919. Thereafter, in peace time, it failed to compete with the commercial lines and it was sold off to the British White Star Line at a loss in 1928. Nevertheless, as a solution to an acute wartime problem, it probably was worth the money.

very critical of Hughes' behaviour at Versailles, decided to become a public focus for the discontent with the Prime Minister. He would contest the safe Melbourne Nationalist seat of Kooyong in the next general election, due in December 1922, on the ticket 'Hughes Must Go'.

A series of episodes had left Hughes particularly vulnerable: his unseemly expulsion of the Labor MP and Sinn Fein sympathiser Hugh Mahon in November 1920 from federal Parliament for disloyalty; his apparent hounding of Justice H B Higgins from the Arbitration Court; an ill-advised acceptance by him of a subscription gift of £25,000 (more than ten times his annual salary) from well-wishers grateful for his War work (half of whom were in Britain); his wife Mary's being created a Dame (GBE) for her charitable work during the War in the New Year's Honours List for 1922; and his failure to establish an enquiry into new states, which was demanded by the Country Party. He was increasingly seen as dictatorial, erratic and corrupt. In truth, he was simply tired and losing touch. Methods which had served him well in wartime were proving unsuitable for the peace.

The general elections of December 1922 yielded a result of 31 Nationals/Liberals, 14 Country, 29 Labor and 1 Independent. This provided an opportunity for a new generation of MPs to exert their influence, men who had served in the fighting forces during the War and who identified Hughes with the old politics of dictatorship, division and corruption. With Page, Bruce and Latham to the fore, and encouraged by Watt, a coalition agreement was forged between the Country Party and Nationalists on the condition that Hughes resign as Prime Minister in favour of the dashing, 40-year-old, returned soldier and Melbourne businessman who was Treasurer, S M Bruce. This duly happened in January 1923 and Hughes retired to the backbenches. He had lost his sense of the mood of the country, as would many a leader before and after him, and he had become a focus for their frustrations. Hughes had had a good run at the top and his remarkable parliamentary career was only half over, but he would never emulate his earlier success.

9

Elder Statesman, 1923–52

Billy Hughes remained in the federal Parliament for nearly 30 more years – the rest of his long life. He had two more tilts at the Prime Ministership, and held a number of Cabinet posts in the 1930s and 1940s. But he would never hold the highest office again. Increasingly, he tended his own legend, defended his legacy and sought to promote causes with which he was already identified. But there were also moments of great drama, indeed revenge and vindication, one great personal tragedy, and occasional flashes of brilliance and insight which recalled his heyday.

On the backbench for the remainder of the 1920s, Hughes occupied himself with his new and safer constituency, North Sydney, to which he had moved from Bendigo in 1922. On the side, he dabbled once more in journalism, undertook a lecture tour to the United States, and wrote a book, *The Splendid Adventure*, part memoir, part analysis, about the British Commonwealth, with special emphasis on Versailles and its aftermath.[1] In Parliament he took the Nationalist whip, supporting the Bruce-Page coalition government, which he argued broadly continued his policies of national development. He did, however, occasionally bridle. In 1924, for instance, he argued that two new cruisers should be built in Australia rather than Britain for reasons of national morale.[2] Three years later, when Bruce finally sold off the Commonwealth Shipping Line, Hughes pointed out that not only was the Bruce-Page government ransoming the economy to the international shipping combine, but they were weakening national defence as some of the ships were part of the auxiliary fleet of the Royal Australian Navy and built for conversion to armed cruisers in time of war.[3]

As the economy grew in the 1920s and the Bruce-Page coalition was returned comfortably in the 1925 elections, Hughes found no opportunity to work his way closer to the levers of power. In 1928–9, however, fortune's wheel turned and he made the most of the new circumstances. First, agricultural prices began to fall and the federal budget deficit became problematic. Then Bruce, who had grown weary of combating the mining and waterside unions, proposed rather quixotically, though with deadly seriousness, that all federal industrial arbitration powers should be transferred to the states forthwith. This was too much for Hughes, who was an architect of the Federal Arbitration Act and saw it as a cornerstone of the state.

Timing his moves with great skill, Hughes crossed the floor with a handful of malcontents, defeating the bill and the government by one vote. Hughes had secured the support of one wobbler by hiding with him in the parliamentary billiards room until the division bell sounded. In the ensuing 1929 election, Bruce suffered the humiliation of losing his own seat, the government were defeated and the Labor Party were returned to power under J H Scullin. Not only had Hughes preserved the federal arbitration system but he had spectacularly turned the tables on his tormentors of 1923.

This double coup gave him immense satisfaction, though he was expelled from the Nationalist Party and compelled to form his own vehicle, the short-lived Australian Party. For a brief few months, with the Bruce government foundering, Hughes imagined his small faction holding the balance of power, and his possibly being kingmaker if not king.[4] It was not to be.

The Great Depression hit Australia hard in the early 1930s. Unemployment approached 30 per cent and the economy shrank by 25 per cent.[5] Always at his best in a crisis, since the middle of 1929 Hughes had confidentially concerted his efforts with Labor's Shadow Treasurer Ted Theodore to advocate a radical proto-Keynesian solution: devalue the currency against sterling, expand the money supply, increase prices and create jobs. Needless to say, he was later a great admirer of Franklin Roosevelt's New Deal. In the event, the Theodore-Hughes programme proved too strong a meat for either the new Labor government or the Nationalist opposition, both of whom were intent on retrenchment, staying on the gold standard and budget balancing. It also looked too much like the debt repudiation being advocated by the followers of Jack Lang, the populist Labor Premier of New South Wales.[6] Eventually, the Scullin federal Labor government split over the issue. In elections in December 1931 Joseph Lyons's new United Australia Party, which included the old Nationalists, won office.

For three years from 1929 Hughes flirted with rejoining the Labor Party. He voted with them to oust Bruce; he collaborated on policy with Theodore, who became federal Treasurer in the new Scullin government; and he voted with them in Parliament throughout 1930. The bitter legacy of conscription was too much for some leading Labor men to forgive however and he never formally re-entered the fold. After the Labor split, he sided with Lyons and accepted the United Australia Party whip.

Lyons recognised Hughes' talents and successively appointed him an Australian delegate to the League of Nations General Assembly in 1932, then Minister for Health and Minister for Repatriation in 1934 and Minister for External Affairs in 1937. During a visit to Europe in 1931–2, Hughes was alerted to the rise of Fascism in Germany and Italy. He was already wary as ever of Japanese expansion in Manchuria. On this trip, probably in his capacity as a board member of AWA, he also tried and failed to buy the Australian rights to John Logie Baird's new invention, television.

As Health Minister Hughes focused on the declining birth-rate and in 1935 supported the George V Jubilee Fund (£250,000) to encourage better maternal practices. He was nick-named the 'Minister for Motherhood' and, linking population decline to defence, called for the country to *populate or perish*.[7] At best, he warned, if something was not done about the birth rate, *we shall be a stagnant people, rotting in the backwater of our own sterility*.[8] The birth-rate picked up with improving economic conditions, but Hughes' campaign also played a modest role. In his capacity as Repatriation Minister, Hughes was instrumental in making war disability pensions more accessible to returned soldiers, whose cause was always close to his heart.

Now in his 70s, by virtue of his position as an elder statesman, as a former war leader, by intellectual conviction and by natural inclination, the 'Little Digger' was ideally placed to play the role of an antipodean Cassandra as the Fascist states geared up for war while the democracies slept. As early as 1933, Hughes published a cold-eyed appraisal in an

American newspaper: *If we want to hold Australia we must be prepared to defend Australia and we know Australia was never so open to attack as she is now. When Britain was mistress of the seas our security was assured. But disquieting news of the British fleet's backwardness shows that, despite all the good will in the world, the British Navy is no longer in a position to come immediately to our aid …We must have an air force, submarines, and surface craft, adequate to patrol our coast lines, and land forces and equipment commensurate to our needs and circumstances.*[9]

> 'If we want to hold Australia we must be prepared to defend Australia and we know Australia was never so open to attack as she is now.'
>
> **BILLY HUGHES, 3 SEPTEMBER 1933**

In July 1934, he published a pamphlet, *The Price of Peace*, to coincide with a government rearmament programme of £40 million over the next three years.[10] In it he argued that the new Singapore naval base, which was under construction, was of questionable use and that a strong air force should be Australia's first line of defence.

A year later Hughes revised and expanded his pamphlet into a book, *Australia and War To-day: The Price of Peace*,[11] in which he wrote that Germany was again intent on world domination. Resolutions by the League of Nations and other international bodies, *unless backed by sanctions … are not only futile but mischievous*. Furthermore, he wrote, *All effective sanctions must be supported by adequate force … Economic sanctions are therefore either an empty gesture, or war*.[12] These words were written before Italy invaded Abyssinia on 3 October 1935. By sheer chance, the book was published on the eve of the introduction of the second reading in the Australian Parliament of a League-inspired sanctions against Italy bill. In early November, Lyons was left no choice but to ask for Hughes's resignation, though after the sanctions had inevitably failed he was also happy to usher Hughes back into Cabinet in late February 1936.

In August 1937 the Hugheses suffered a devastating personal tragedy. Their daughter Helen, now aged 22 and unmarried, had fallen pregnant, and in February had been hurried off on a prolonged holiday to Britain to have her child in seclusion. Helen died in a London private hospital of complications following a caesarean section, though her baby son David survived. He was adopted by Vincent Duffy of the Australian High Commission in London and still lives in Sydney. Hughes left him £5,000 in his will.[13]

Hughes's relations with his older children had been distant and somewhat chequered for over 20 years. Arthur became a public accountant in Sydney, William studied agriculture and became a public servant in Canberra, and Charles a wool classer in Auckland, New Zealand. Ethel married and lived first in Sydney and later in California; Dolly remained single in Melbourne; and Lily, a lifetime invalid, lived in Christchurch, New Zealand. Hughes regularly sent his daughters modest sums of money. In the mid-1920s, however, he had a major falling out with Ethel who threatened to go public about his supposed ill-treatment of his illegitimate children if he did not arrive at a permanent financial settlement for them. An accommodation was reached; but thereafter Hughes remained estranged from Ethel, though he still saw his other children occasionally, bearing gifts for them and his grandchildren. All his children were treated fairly in his will.[14] Also significant was Edith Haynes, his wife's niece, who lived for many years with the Hugheses and stayed on with Dame Mary after Billy Hughes died.[15]

After Helen's death, Hughes escaped his private demons by throwing himself into his work. When Lyons' United Australia Party won another general election in October 1937, Hughes was made Minister for External Affairs; though in the absence of an Australian diplomatic corps of any significance, Lyons kept relations with the Great Powers in his own hands and those of the High Commissioner in London, Bruce, who answered to him. It fell to Hughes, however, to comment on Germany's and Italy's colonial claims. Meeting them, he said, inimitably, would be *like giving a snack of sandwiches to a hungry tiger – it would only sharpen their appetite.*[16] Later, on a visit to New Guinea, he said, *On this rock we have got our mandate and have built our church, and all hell is not going to take it away from us. This territory has a great future and what we have we shall hold.*[17] This drew protests from Dr Rudolf Asmis, the German Consul-General in Sydney. Needless to say, Hughes was unrepentant.

The Munich Agreement (1938), hailed by Lyons as a success for appeasement, was seen by Hughes as offering a mere breathing space. He was delighted, however, when Lyons, to stave off cries for conscription, asked him to head a national recruitment drive to double the size of the militia to 70,000, a figure he achieved within three months.

Lyons' unexpected death in office in April 1939 led to a succession struggle. Hughes stood against the heir apparent Robert Menzies and two other Cabinet members, Richard Casey and Thomas White. Bruce initially stood in the wings, then ruled himself out by insisting on a national coalition. Casey and White were eliminated in the preliminary party room ballot, and Menzies pipped Hughes to the post by only four (some sources say two) votes. Remarkably, at 77 years of age Hughes had barely missed out on the Prime Ministership again. Menzies made him Attorney-General and Deputy Prime Minister. But this was his last hurrah.

During the Second World War, Hughes made himself useful without getting too embroiled in high political intrigue. He settled a coal strike, organised clandestine funding for loyalist unionists and oversaw the banning of the Communist Party during its anti-war phase. He also had stints as Industry Minister and as Navy Minister. Menzies was overthrown by his own party in August 1941, to be replaced briefly by the Country Party's Arthur Fadden, before Labor came to office under John Curtin in October. Hughes chortled that Menzies *couldn't lead a flock of homing pigeons.*[18] In the New Year's Honours List for 1941 Hughes, who for political reasons had rejected knighthoods and a peerage in the past, was delighted to be made a Companion of Honour. After Menzies' fall, he became caretaker leader of the United Australia Party, but he was replaced by a rehabilitated Menzies in August 1943. Hughes enjoyed serving as a senior statesman on Curtin's Advisory War Council and was delighted when Curtin, an arch-anti-conscriptionist in the First World War, successfully persuaded his Labor government and party to introduce conscription in the Second.

For Australia, the Second World War began like the First, fighting in the Middle East to defend the Suez Canal; but once Japan entered the war in December 1941, Australia's forces were almost totally focused on meeting the Japanese threat in the Pacific. Much of the fighting took place in New Guinea. Hughes had the grim satisfaction of seeing the war against Japan that he had envisaged for 40 years finally happen. Curtin's introduction of conscription was designed to help repel the Japanese. If some thought that Australia's First World War was more a war of Empire than one of national survival, none could say that of the Second when there was an ever present threat of invasion.

Mercurial to the end, Hughes refused Menzies' request to leave the Advisory War Council in 1944 only to be expelled from the United Australia Party; though he joined Menzies' new Liberal Party soon afterwards. When, at Hughes's 88th (really 90th) birthday party in Parliament in 1952, Menzies, again Prime Minister, quipped that there was not a party Hughes had not been expelled from, Fadden interjected that he had not been thrown out of his party, the Country Party, to which the nonagenarian riposted without a moment's hesitation, *No ... had to draw the line somewhere, didn't I?*[19]

After the war, Hughes fought and won his North Sydney seat (1946); then, after an increase in the size of the House of Representatives, the neighbouring Bradfield seat in two more federal elections (1949, and 1951). But he remained on the backbenches. In these twilight years, he dictated two extremely colourful and entertaining volumes of memoirs, *Crusts and Crusades* (1947) and *Policies and Potentates* (1950). At the time of his death from pneumonia on 28 October 1952, he was preparing to speak in Parliament against the sale of the government's share in the Commonwealth Oil Refineries, the last of his quangos. The share in Amalgamated Wireless (Australasia) had been withdrawn a few years earlier. He had been 58 years an Australian MP, state and federal, and had sat in every Commonwealth Parliament since federation. His state funeral at St Andrew's (Anglican) Cathedral in Sydney was the largest the city had ever seen. Before it, the public filed past his coffin for two days and two nights.

The sound, fury and controversy are now long gone. Every Anzac Day in Sydney a chair is placed near the Cenotaph opposite the General Post Office in Martin Place and on it is placed Billy's slouch hat, the same as worn by the First AIF and its successors. The 'Little Digger' still greets and is remembered by his beloved Anzacs and through them grateful Australians across the generations.

Conclusion

If politics is the art of the possible, then Billy Hughes strained the possible to previously unexpected limits. Starting from a very humble background, by sheer talent and determination, and using the full mix of law, cajolery and threats he had honed as a trade union leader battling for a 'log of claims',[1] he rose to the summit of Australian and Imperial politics, the top of the British world. He was instrumental in forming a genuinely effective political party for the labouring classes, the world's first. He was one of the inventors of Australia's federal industrial arbitration system. He secured viable markets for Australia's key primary industries under extremely difficult wartime conditions. He shaped Australia's fledgling defence forces and made them strong. He was godfather to Australia's iron, steel and processed metals industries, its aviation, radio, government laboratories and much else. What was his 'war socialism' to some was nation-building enterprise to others. He represented his country at the seat of Empire and in the Empire's councils so well that he was offered a seamless translation into the British Parliament. Internationally, at Versailles, his politicking was effective enough to win for Australia and the British Empire control of the strategically vital German New Guinea and the resource-rich island of Nauru. His audacity and brink-manship safeguarded 'White Australia' against a Japanese challenge. He failed to win significant reparations, but then so did everyone else.

At home, he had failed by a whisker to introduce conscription for overseas service by direct democratic means. It would have been another world first had he brought it off. Though he left the body politic bruised, post-war Australians were better off materially and the nation was in a relatively sound strategic position. Nevertheless, Hughes' dictatorial methods and abrasiveness, useful in war, proved a liability in peace. The whirligig of time (and circumstance), whose momentum he had exploited to rise up, eventually flung him down as he failed to anticipate its next gyration.

Hughes assiduously cultivated his own legend as a lone but successful battler against the odds, defying at first Sydney's capitalists, then all of Australia's establishment, then Lloyd George, the Japanese, and ultimately Woodrow Wilson and *the whole civilized world*. The truth, however, is more intriguing and more believable.

None of Hughes' achievements came without significant support from others. He helped refashion political labour in Australia after the titanic struggle of the 1890s strikes. Labour's raw power pre-dated him, but he helped focus it for its next phase. He also lost its support when it moved into the 'direct action' militancy of the later War years. Rhetoric, suasion and conjuring would only go so far.

He was successful over obtaining the Pacific island Mandates because Britain, France, Japan, Italy, his fellow Dominions and ultimately even the United States were behind him. Similarly, over 'White Australia', he was a catspaw for South

Africa, Canada and again for the United States whose representatives cynically manoeuvred him into taking the blame. On total reparations, where despite being egged on by the French and others, his proved to be a lone voice among the main delegates and he had no success at all. Hughes' David only prevailed over Goliath when he had powerful legions behind him and, more important, Goliath was willing to go along with the act. He had the wit and perception to grasp his opportunities and to put the best light on the outcomes.

Billy Hughes was rude, irascible, secretive and of changing party and personal loyalties, creating a series of power bases only to abandon each in turn when he failed adequately to tend them and they fell apart under him. Yet, he was also highly effective in the service of his nation and Empire, a complementary service in which he never wavered. In the last analysis, Hughes was both nationalist and Imperialist, arguing for Australia's interests with the clout of the British Empire behind him. In this he was quintessentially a man of his time, characteristic of Australia's, and indeed all the Dominions', Britannic moment. The British Empire literally made him and in so doing he and it did much to make modern Australia.

Notes

Introduction

1. Successively, Donald Horne, *In Search of Billy Hughes* (Macmillan, London: 1979); Malcolm Booker, *The Great Professional: A Study of W. M. Hughes* (McGraw-Hill, Sydney: 1980); and L F Fitzhardinge, *William Morris Hughes: A Political Biography*, 2 Vols, *Vol. 1 That Fiery Particle, 1862–1914,* and *Vol. 2 The Little Digger, 1914–1952* (Angus & Robertson, Sydney: 1964, 1979). I omit Aneurin Hughes, *Billy Hughes, Prime Minister and Controversial Founding Father of the Australian Labor Party* (Wiley, Brisbane: 2005), which is amusing and chatty but sometimes unreliable. Earlier noteworthy biographies include W Farmer Whyte, *William Morris Hughes* (Angus and Robertson, Sydney: 1957) and Frank Browne, *They Called Him Billy* (Peter Hudson, Sydney: 1946).

2. W J Hudson, *Billy Hughes in Paris: The Birth of Australian Diplomacy* (Nelson, Melbourne: 1979); Peter Spartalis, *The Diplomatic Battles of Billy Hughes* (Hale & Iremonger, Sydney: 1983); Neville Meaney, *The Search for Security in the Pacific, 1901–1914* (Sydney

University Press, Sydney: 1976) and *Australia and World Crisis, 1914–1923* (Sydney University Press, Sydney: 2009).

3. E M Andrews, *The Anzac Illusion: Anglo-Australian Relations during World War I* (Cambridge University Press, Melbourne: 1993).

4. Carl Bridge and Kent Fedorowich, eds, *The British World: Diaspora, Culture and Identity* (Frank Cass, London: 2003); P A Buckner and Douglas Francis, eds, *Rediscovering the British World* (University of Calgary Press, Calgary: 2005) and *Canada and the British World* (University of British Columbia Press, Vancouver: 2007); Simon Potter, *News and the British World* (Clarendon, Oxford: 2003); and Gary Magee and Andrew Thompson, *Empire and Globalisation: Networks of People, Goods and Capital in the British World c. 1850–1914* (Cambridge University Press, Cambridge: 2010).

1: New South Welshman, 1862–1901

1. Booker, *Great Professional*, pp 3–6.

2. Whyte, *Hughes*, p 5.

3. The last lines of Henry Lawson's poem, 'The Roaring Days' (1889).

4. Diary entry, 8 December 1898, A G Austin, ed., *The Webbs' Australian Diary 1898* (Pitman, Melbourne: 1965) p 108.

5. William Lane's novel, *The Workingman's Paradise* (1892) was published in the immediate aftermath of the Great Strikes. The title was meant to be ironical but the description stuck and was read popularly as a faithful description when times improved.

6. Manning Clark, ed., *Select Documents in Australian History, Vol. II, 1851–1900* (Angus & Robertson, Sydney: 1977) pp 257, 667.
7. Clark, *Select Documents*, p 257.
8. Horne, *Search*, p 26.
9. Horne, *Search*, p 52.
10. *Sydney Morning Herald*, 26 July 1898.
11. *Daily Telegraph* (Sydney), 5 July 1895.
12. W M Hughes, *Policies and Potentates* (Angus & Robertson, Sydney: 1950) pp 37–41.
13. Henry Gullett cited in Fitzhardinge, *Hughes*, Vol. 1, p 107.
14. *NSW Parliamentary Debates*, 18 October 1899.
15. *NSW Parliamentary Debates*, 21 March 1899.

2: Nation-building and Troubleshooting, 1901–14

1. Paul Kelly, *The End of Certainty* (Allen & Unwin, Sydney: 1992).
2. *Commonwealth of Australia Parliamentary Debates*, 12 September 1901; hereafter *CPD*.
3. *CPD*, 21 July 1903.
4. *CPD*, 12 August 1904. Booker, *Great Professional*, p 112.
5. Fitzhardinge, *Hughes*, Vol. 1, Ch. IX.
6. Cited in Fitzhardinge, *Hughes*, Vol. 1, pp 188, 190.
7. Cited in Fitzhardinge, *Hughes*, Vol. 1, p 192.
8. *Sydney Morning Herald*, 20 February 1909.
9. *Daily Telegraph* (Sydney), 4 December 1909.
10. Fitzhardinge, *Hughes*, Vol. 1, pp 237–9.
11. The Russians lost all eight of their battleships in the battle, the Japanese none.
12. Meaney, *Search for Security*, Ch. 5.
13. *CPD*, 7 October 1909.

14. P Dennis *et al.*, eds, *The Oxford Companion to Australian Military History* (Oxford University Press, Melbourne: 1995) p 175. See also Craig Wilcox, *For Hearths and Homes: Citizen Soldiering in Australia 1854–1945* (Allen & Unwin, Sydney: 1998); John Barrett, *Falling In: Australians and 'Boy' Conscription 1911–1915* (Hale & Iremonger, Sydney: 1979); and Thomas W Tanner, *Compulsory Citizen Soldiers* (APCOL, Sydney: 1980).

15. Alan Stephens, *The Royal Australian Navy: A History* (Oxford University Press, Melbourne: 2001) Ch. 1.

16. *CPD*, 26 June 1912.

17. Gavin Souter, *Acts of Parliament* (Melbourne University Press, Melbourne: 1988) p 98; *Sydney Morning Herald*, 11 April 1910.

18. *CPD*, 27 May 1909.

19. Cited in Souter, *Acts*, p 120.

20. *Bulletin*, 20 February 1913.

21. The Parliament moved to the permanent capital Canberra in 1927.

22. E Hughes to W M Hughes, 14 August 1906, cited in Fitzhardinge, *Hughes*, Vol. 1, p 178.

3: War, 1914–16

1. Meaney, *Crisis*, p 21.

2. *Argus* (Melbourne), 1 August 1914. The phrase dates back to Empire Day, 1907, when it was used by W W Oakes, a New South Wales state MP, Andrews, *Anzac Illusion*, p 35.

3. Ernest Scott, *Australia During the War* (University of Queensland Press, Brisbane: 1989, 1st pub. 1936) p 54.

4. Sir John Latham, 'Sir Robert Garran – An Appreciation', *Australian Law Journal*, Vol. 30 (1957), p 495.

5. Fitzhardinge, *Hughes*, Vol. 2, p 19.

6. Fitzhardinge, *Hughes*, Vol. 2, pp 18–26; Scott, *War*, Ch. XV; and Peter Cochrane, *Industrialization and Dependence: Australia's Road to Economic Development, 1870–1939* (University of Queensland Press, Brisbane: 1980) pp 76–8.

7. The best discussion is in Kosmas Tsokhas, *Markets, Money and Empire: The Political Economy of the Australian Wool Industry* (Melbourne University Press, Melbourne: 1990) Ch. 1.

8. Herbert Hoover, the United States wartime food controller, estimated that 5,000 tons of wheat required 15,000 tons of shipping from Australia, 10,000 from Argentina and 5,000 from North America; Scott, *War*, p 333.

9. Scott, *War*, Chs XIV and XVII.

10. Hughes' speech, Sydney Town Hall, 4 April 1917, Hughes Papers, 1538/28/70, National Library of Australia [NLA], Canberra.

11. Scott, *War*, pp 523–6.

12. Bernard Attard, 'Politics, Finance and Anglo-Australian Relations: Australian Borrowing in London, 1914–1920', *Australian Journal of Politics and History*, Vol. 35, No. 2 (1989) pp 142–63.

13. Scott, *War*, Ch. XIII; *Official Year Book of the Commonwealth of Australia, 1919* (Government Printer, Melbourne) p 756; A G L Shaw, *Economic Development of Australia* (Longman Green, Melbourne: 3rd edition, 1955) Ch. XV. The Commonwealth's public works

expenditure figures are difficult to ascertain as the reporting is obscure and varies from year to year.

14. Scott, *War*, Ch. XXI.

15. W M Hughes, 'The Call to Arms', 15 December 1915, reproduced in Frank Crowley, ed., *Modern Australia in Documents, Vol. 1, 1901–1939* (Wren, Melbourne: 1973) pp 249–50.

16. Scott, *War*, pp 310–11.

17. Cited in Scott, *War*, p 310.

18. Fitzhardinge, *Hughes*, Vol. 2, pp 38–41.

19. Fitzhardinge, *Hughes*, Vol. 2, pp 48–56.

20. G Sawer, *The Federal Government and the Law, 1901–1929* (Melbourne University Press, Melbourne: 1956) p 151.

21. Munro Ferguson to Bonar Law, 4 August and 8 November 1915, to Birdwood, 13 January 1919, all cited in Fitzhardinge, *Hughes*, Vol. 2, pp 47–8.

22. Fisher's phrase, cited in Fitzhardinge, *Hughes*, Vol. 2, p 76.

23. *The Times*, 10 March 1916.

24. Fitzhardinge, *Hughes*, Vol. 2, Chs IV–VI; Hughes, *Policies and Potentates*, pp 195–8.

25. *Bulletin*, 16 March 1916.

26. Fitzhardinge, *Hughes*, Vol. 2, pp 137–44; Scott, *War*, Ch. XVIII.

27. Meaney, *Crisis*, pp 143–8, 248–55; Ian Nish, *Alliance in Decline: A Study in Anglo-Japanese Relations, 1908–23* (Athlone, London: 1972) is excellent on the British background.

28. See Paul Baker, *King and Country Call: New Zealanders, Conscription and the Great War* (Auckland University Press, Auckland: 1988) pp 86–95; F W

Perry, *The Commonwealth Armies: Manpower
and Organisation in Two World Wars* (Manchester
University Press, Manchester: 1988) Chs 1, 4–6.

4: The Battle for Conscription, 1916–18

1. Cited in Souter, *Acts*, p 147.
2. Fitzhardinge suggests Anderson acted alone, *Hughes*,
   Vol. 2, pp 182–5. If so, he read Hughes's mind perfectly.
3. L C Jauncey, *The Story of Conscription* (Macmillan,
   Melbourne: 1968 edn) Chs 4 and 5.
4. Cited in Fitzhardinge, *Hughes*, Vol. 2, pp 175, 179.
5. Cited in Fitzhardinge, *Hughes*, Vol. 2, p 178.
6. For a full account, see Ian Turner, *Sydney's Burning*
   (Heinemann, Melbourne: 1967).
7. Cited in Fitzhardinge, *Hughes*, Vol. 2, p 217; Mannix's
   speech at Clifton Hill, Victoria, 16 September 1916,
   cited in E J Brady, *Doctor Mannix: Archbishop of
   Melbourne* (Library of National Biography, Melbourne:
   1934) p 61.
8. There is a good selection, including those cited below,
   in J M Main, ed., *Conscription: The Australian Debate,
   1901–1970* (Cassell, Melbourne: 1970).
9. The sinking of the passenger liner *Lusitania* by a
   German submarine in May 1915 was one of the
   incidents which helped in the United States' decision to
   enter the War in April 1917. Edith Cavell was a British
   nurse executed by German firing squad in Belgium in
   October 1915.
10. Hughes to Murdoch, 4 November 1916, and Hughes
    to Bonar Law, 6 November 1916, cited in Fitzhardinge,
    Hughes, Vol. 2, pp 213, and 215.

11. Cited in Stephen Murray-Smith, 'On the Conscription Trail: The Second Referendum Seen From Beside W M Hughes', *Labour History*, No. 33 (1977), p 101.

12. Glenn Withers, 'The 1916–17 Conscription Referenda: A Cliometric Reappraisal', *Historical Studies*, Vol. 20, No. 78 (1982) pp 36–47.

13. John Hirst, 'Labor and the Great War' in Robert Manne, ed., *The Australian Century: Political Struggle in the Building of a Nation* (Text, Melbourne: 1999) pp 55–6. The information on Catholic enlistment is from Professors Peter Dennis and Jeffrey Grey and the AIF database project at the Australian Defence Academy, Canberra.

14. Secretary of State for Colonies to Hughes, cable, 1 December 1917, Hughes Papers, 1538/20/277. Scott puts the figure higher at 420,000, *War*, pp 407–9.

15. Perry, *Commonwealth Armies,* Ch. 9; Carl Bridge, 'Australia's and Canada's Wars, 1914–18 and 1939–45: Some Reflections', *Round Table*, No. 361 (2001), pp 623–32.

16. B H Liddell Hart, *History of the First World War* (Pan, London: 1970) pp 362–4.

17. Scott, *War*, p. 665. Ian Turner, *Industrial Labour and Politics* (Australian National University Press, Canberra: 1965).

18. *Argus* (Melbourne), 11–12 December 1917.

19. Mannix's speech opening a new school on Brunswick, Victoria, January 1917, Michael Gilchrist, *Daniel Mannix* (Freedom Publishing, Melbourne: 2004) pp 41–3; Niall Brennan, *Dr Mannix* (Angus & Robertson, London: 1965) pp 153–4; 'Mr Hughes replies

to Dr Mannix', n. d., December 1917, Hughes Papers, 1538/20/576–7.

5: Man of Empire, 1918

1. Hughes to Munro Ferguson, 25 April 1918, Novar Papers, 696/2717, NLA, Canberra.
2. David Low, *The Billy Book: Hughes Abroad* (NSW Bookstall Co., Sydney: 1918).
3. Low, *Billy Book*, p 41.
4. David Low, *Low's Autobiography* (Michael Joseph, London: 1956) p 70.
5. Fitzhardinge, *Hughes*, Vol. 2, pp 313–14.
6. Hughes to Pearce, 2 June 1918, Pearce Collection, 3/3, Australian War Memorial, Canberra.
7. Reading to Balfour and Long, cable, 2 June 1918, Balfour Papers, Add. 49741, Fol. 200, British Library.
8. Hughes, *Policies and Potentates*, p 229.
9. Spartalis, *Diplomatic Battles*, p 59.
10. Murdoch to Hughes, 22 November 1917, Hughes Papers, 1538/20/343.
11. Speech to a Representative Body of American citizens [the Pilgrim Club], n. d. [1 June] 1918, Hughes Papers, 1538/23/2977.
12. Hughes to Watt, 3 June 1918, CP 360/9/1, National Archives of Australia [NAA], Canberra.
13. See Carl Bridge, 'Relations with the United States' in C Bridge and B Attard, eds, *Between Empire and Nation* (Australian Scholarly Publishing, Melbourne: 2001) pp 178–9.
14. W M Hughes, *The Splendid Adventure: A Review of Empire Relations* (Ernest Benn, London: 1929), p 78.

15. This and the preceding paragraph: Imperial War Cabinet Minutes, 28 June 1918, 23, 25, 30 July 1918, 14 August 1918, 11 October 1918, Hughes Papers, 1538/23/3/730–33.
16. 'Mr Hughes' Speech at Queen's Hall Today', Hughes Papers, 1538/23/5/34/22818–24.
17. Fitzhardinge, *Hughes*, Vol. 2, pp 329–33
18. Long to Hughes, 10 October 1918, Hughes Papers, 1538/23/178.
19. Hughes to Munro Ferguson, 28 September 1918, cited in Avner Offer, *The First World War: An Agrarian Interpretation* (Oxford University Press, Oxford: 1989) p 368.
20. Scott, *War*, p 589; *Argus* (Melbourne), 5 May 1917.
21. Scott, *War*, pp 590–1.
22. Scott, *War*, pp 529–40, 595–7; Fitzhardinge, *Hughes*, Vol. 2, p 336.
23. Scott, *War*, Chs XIV-XVI; Tsokhas, *Markets, Money and Empire*, Chs 1–3.
24. D B Copland, 'Australia in the World War: Economic', Ch. XIX Pt III in J Holland Rose *et al.*, eds, *Cambridge History of the British Empire, Vol. 7, Part I: Australia* (Cambridge University Press, Cambridge: 1933). See also Marnie Haig-Muir, 'The Economy at War', Ch. 4 in Joan Beaumont, ed., *Australia's War, 1914–18* (Allen & Unwin, Sydney: 1995); F Carrigan, 'The Imperial Struggle for Control of the Broken Hill Base-Metal Industry, 1914–1915' in E L Wheelwright and Ken Buckley, eds, *Essays in the Political Economy of Australian Capitalism*, Vol. 5 (ANZ Book Co, Sydney: 1983) pp 164–86; and P Richardson, 'The Origins of the

Collins House Group, 1915–51', *Australian Economic History Review*, Vol. 27, No. 1 (1987) pp 3–29.

25. Hughes to Watt, cable, 16 October 1918, Hughes Papers, 1538/23/227.

26. Hughes to Watt, cable, 23 October 1918, Hughes Papers, 1538/23/236.

27. *The Times*, 8, 9 November 1918.

28. Imperial War Cabinet Minutes, 5 November 1918, Hughes Papers, 1538/23/734.

29. Imperial War Cabinet Minutes, 26 November 1918.

30. Imperial War Cabinet Minutes, 30 December 1918, Hughes Papers, 1538/23/730–33.

31. Imperial War Cabinet Minutes, 26 November 1918, Hughes Papers, 1538/23/30–33.

32. Imperial War Cabinet, Committee on Indemnity, Cab. 27/43/9188, The National Archives [TNA], Kew, London; Imperial War Cabinet Minutes, 24 December 1918, Hughes Papers, 1538/23/734.

33. D Lloyd George, *The Truth about the Peace Treaties*, Vol. 1 (Gollancz, London: 1938) p 461. Hudson, *Hughes*, p 36.

34. Sir George Foster, quoted in Margaret MacMillan, *Peacemakers* (John Murray, London: 2003) p 198.

35. Cited in Hudson, *Hughes*, pp 36–7.

36. Hughes to Lloyd George, 4 November 1918, cited in Fitzhardinge, *Hughes*, Vol. 2, pp 348–9.

37. Imperial War Cabinet Minutes, 5, 2, 21, 26 November, 31 December 1918, Hughes Papers, 1538/23/730–33. Meaney, *Crisis*, Chs 3, 4 and 10.

38. Note by Secretary of the Imperial War Cabinet, 13 January 1919, Hughes Papers, 1538/24/13. Fitzhardinge, *Hughes*, Vol. 2, pp 362–9.

6: Peacemaking, 1919

1. Hughes, *Splendid Adventure*, p 237.
2. Winston Churchill, *The World Crisis: The Aftermath* (Butterworth, London: 1929) p 152.
3. Cited in Fitzhardinge, *Hughes*, Vol. 2, p 391.
4. United States Department of State, *Foreign Relations of the United States [FRUS]: Papers relating to the Paris Peace Conference, 1919* 13 Vols, (Washington, State Department, 1942–7) Vol. III, pp 718–22, 738–43, 749, 763–71.
5. Cited in Hudson, *Hughes*, p 20.
6. *Herald* (Melbourne), 27 January 1919.
7. Eggleston Diary, 27 January 1919, Document 14 in Hudson, *Hughes*, p 116.
8. Appendix to Minutes of a Meeting of the British Empire delegation, 29 January 1919, Cook Papers, 762, NLA, Canberra. See Hudson, *Hughes*, pp 135–6, for a note about attribution.
9. Cited in Scott, *War*, p 784.
10. Fitzhardinge, *Hughes*, Vol. 2, p 392.
11. *FRUS*, Vol. III, p 786.
12. Fitzhardinge, *Hughes*, Vol. 2, p 396; Lloyd George, *Peace Treaties*, Vol. 1, p 542.
13. Fitzhardinge, *Hughes*, Vol. 2, p 396.
14. *FRUS*, Vol. III, pp 799–800; Auchinloss Diary, 30 January 1919, cited in Fizhardinge, *Hughes*, Vol. 2, p 394; Lord Riddell, *Intimate Diary of the Peace Conference and After, 1919–1923* (Gollancz, London: 1933) p 17.
15. *FRUS*, Vol. III, pp 396–7.
16. Stephen Bonsal, *Suitors and Suppliants* (Prentice-Hall, New York: 1946) p 229.

17. Cited in Bonsal, *Suitors*, p 398.
18. Scott, *War*, pp 788–9.
19. Fitzhardinge, *Hughes*, Vol. 2, p 398.
20. Hughes to Watt, cable, 13 April 1919, CP 290/3/1, NAA, Canberra.
21. The best discussion is in Spartalis, *Diplomatic Battles*, Ch. 8.
22. Eggleston Papers, 423/6/69 *et seq.*, NLA, Canberra.
23. Hughes note, n.d., Hughes Papers, 1538/24.2/902. Emphasis in the original.
24. Hughes, *Policies and Potentates*, p 247.
25. Cited in full in Fitzhardinge, *Hughes*, Vol. 2, pp 407–9.
26. Spartalis, *Diplomatic Battles*, p 188.
27. Hughes to Watt, cable, 17 April 1919, CP 360/8/4, NAA, Canberra.
28. Harold Nicolson, *Peacemaking 1919* (Constable, London: 1933) p 145.
29. House Diary, 13 February 1919, cited in MacMillan, *Peacemakers*, p 329.

7: Dividing the Spoils, 1919

1. Recorded in Latham Diary, 13 February 1919, Latham Papers, 1009/21/1409, NLA, Canberra.
2. Reparations Commission minutes, reproduced in P M Burnett, ed., *Reparations at the Peace Conference*, 2 Vols (Columbia University Press, New York: 1940).
3. T W Lamont, 'Reparations' in E M House and C Seymour, eds, *What Really Happened at Paris: The Story of the Peace Conference* (C. Scribner's Sons, New York: 1921) pp 269–70.
4. British Empire delegation minutes, 13 March 1919, CP 351/1/B4, NAA, Canberra.

5. Hughes to Lloyd George, 11 April 1919, Lloyd George Papers, F28/3/26, House of Lords, London.

6. Lloyd George to Hughes, 14 April 1919, Lloyd George Papers, F28/3/27.

7. Hughes to Watt, cable, 4 May 1919, CP360/8/4, NAA, Canberra.

8. Hughes to Munro Ferguson, 17 May 1919, Novar Papers, 696/2798–2800. Emphasis in the original.

9. Spartalis, *Diplomatic Battles*, pp 167–8.

10. Hughes and Peace Conference, n. d., Hughes Papers, 1538/863/folder 11; Balfour of Burleigh to Hughes, 16 September 1918, Garran Papers, CP 351/1/6, NAA, Canberra; Scott, *War*, p 797.

11. Memorandum by Milner to British Empire delegation, 13 March 1919, Garran Papers, CP 360/8/4, NAA, Canberra; Memorandum by Hughes to British Empire delegation, c. 18 March 1919, Hughes Papers, 1538/24/60.

12. Hughes to Milner, 3 May 1919, Hughes Papers, 1538/24/136.

13. Watt to Hughes, cable, 9 May 1919, Hughes to Watt, cable, 4 June 1919, CP 360/8/4, NAA, Canberra.

14. Agreement regarding Nauru between His Majesty's Governments in Great Britain, Australia and New Zealand, 2 June 1919, Hughes Papers, 1538/24.2/1008–12; Scott, *War*, p 800, fn 79.

15. Hughes and Peace Conference, n.d., Hughes Papers, 1538/863.2/folder 11.

16. Lord Hankey, *The Supreme Control at the Paris Peace Conference 1919*, Vol. 1 (Allen and Unwin, London: 1963) p 45.

17. Imperial War Cabinet Minutes, 26 November 1918, Hughes Papers, 1538/23/730–33.
18. Imperial War Cabinet Minutes, 30 December 1918, Hughes Papers, 1538/23/734.
19. Hughes, 'Notes', 21 March 1919, CP351/1/B4, NAA, Canberra. See also David Hunter Miller, *My Diary at the Conference of Paris with Documents*, Vol. VII (Appeal Printing Company, New York: 1924) pp 240–6.
20. *Sydney Morning Herald*, 23 June 1919.
21. Cited in Hudson, *Hughes*, p 76.
22. Robert Garran, *Prosper the Commonwealth* (Angus & Robertson, Sydney: 1958) p 271.
23. Cited in Souter, *Acts*, pp 171–2.
24. It was approved rather than formally ratified, as ratification was the King's prerogative.
25. *CPD*, 10 September 1919.
26. *CPD*, 10 September 1919.
27. *CPD*, 10 September 1919.

8: On Top of the British World? 1919–23

1. Notes of a Meeting of Representatives of the United Kingdom, the Dominions and India, 21 June 1921, Hughes Papers, 1538/25/425.
2. *CPD*, 7 April 1921.
3. Notes of Meetings of Ministers and Prime Ministers of the British Empire, 29 June, 11 and 27 July 1921, Hughes Papers, 1538/25/440–1, 474, 642.
4. Notes of Meetings of the Prime Ministers of the British Empire, Hughes Papers, 19, 20, 29 July 1919, 1538/25/111–15, 266–9, 272–7, 332–41.
5. Notes of Meetings of the Prime Ministers of the British Empire, 19, 20, 23, 29 July 1921, Hughes Papers,

1538/25, 111–15, 266–9, 322–7. Hughes pointed out on 19 July that Britain spent £1–18s-8 1/2d per capita on defence, Australia 15s-4 1/2d, New Zealand 4s-4 1/2d, South Africa 3s-5 1/2d and Canada 1s-6d.

6. Hughes to Cook, 6 August 1921, CP103/3/1, NAA, Canberra.

7. Notes of Meetings of the Prime Ministers of the British Empire, 5 July 1921, Hughes Papers, 1538/25/454.

8. Notes of Meetings of the Prime Ministers of the British Empire, 12 July 1921, Hughes Papers, 1538/25/475.

9. Pearce to Hughes, 13 June 1919, Hughes Papers, 1538/24.1/402.

10. Notes of Meetings of the Prime Ministers of the British Empire, 12 and 13 July 1921, and Churchill to Hughes, 13 July 1921, Hughes Papers, 1538/25/85–6, 250–7, 263–5, 1201. Fitzhardinge, *Hughes*, Vol. 2, pp 4377–8. Hughes was supported by Sir Ross Smith, the aviator, who was now the Vickers agent in Australia. Vickers manufactured both the aircraft and the airships in question.

11. Notes of Meetings of the Prime Ministers of the British Empire, 2 August 1921, Hughes Papers, 1538/25/644.

12. Notes of Meetings of the Prime Ministers of the British Empire, 5 July, 1–2 August 1921, Hughes Papers, 1538/25/349–50, 644; Fitzhardinge, *Hughes*, Vol. 2, pp 478–9.

13. Anglo-Persian Oil Company to Hughes, 26 June 1919, 7 July 1921, Marsh to Deane, 26 July 1921, Hughes Papers, 1538/24/324–5, /25/64–9, 144–8.

14. Michael Roe, *Australia, Britain and Migration, 1915–1940* (Cambridge University Press, Melbourne: 1995) Ch. 2, is the best account.

15. *CPD*, 26 July 1922. Meaney, *Crisis*, p 499.
16. Carl Bridge, 'Australia's Refusal to Send Troops to Mesopotamia, September 1920: A Note', *Journal of Australian Studies*, Vol. 9 (1981) pp 71–6.
17. The latest account is Paul R. Bartrop, *Bolt from the Blue* (Halstead Press, Sydney: 2002).

9: Elder Statesman, 1923–52

1. (Ernest Benn, London: 1929).
2. *CPD*, 11, 12 September 1924.
3. *CPD*, 9 November 1927; Whyte, *Hughes*, pp 460–1.
4. The best account is still Warren Denning, *Caucus Crisis: The Rise and Fall of the Scullin Government* (Cumberland Argus, Parramatta: 1937; republished by Hale & Iremonger, Sydney: 1992).
5. Vamplew, ed., *Australians: Historical Statistics*, pp 133, 152.
6. Fitzhardinge, *Hughes*, Vol. 2, pp 588–90.
7. *Argus*, 6 March 1935.
8. Cited in Fitzhardinge, *Hughes*, Vol. 2, p 630.
9. *New York American*, 3 September 1933.
10. Published under the auspices of 'The Defense of Australia League'. On re-armament, see Andrew May, 'Fortress Australia', Ch. 12 in Bridge and Attard, eds, *Between Empire and Nation*.
11. (Angus & Robertson, Sydney: 1935).
12. Hughes, *Australia and War To-day*, pp 84, 94–5.
13. Aneurin Hughes, *Hughes*, Ch. 13.
14. Aneurin Hughes, *Hughes*, pp 88–93, 159–60; Whyte, *Hughes*, appendix II.
15. After Billy's death, Dame Mary sold the marital house in Lindfield, Sydney, and moved across the harbour to a

flat at Darling Point where she lived with Edith Haynes
until her death in 1958; Aneurin Hughes, *Hughes*, p 155.
16. *Sydney Morning Herald*, 25 26 January 1938.
17. *Sydney Morning Herald*, 4 June 1938.
18. S. Murray-Smith, *The Dictionary of Australian Quotations* (Heinemann, Melbourne: 1984, 1987) p 122.
19. Fitzhardinge, *Hughes*, Vol. 2, p 670.

Conclusion

1. 'Log of claims' is a technical legal phrase for the new wage rates and working conditions an industrial advocate tries to gain for the members of a trade union in a hearing before an industrial court or tribunal.

Chronology

YEAR	AGE	THE LIFE AND THE LAND
1862	0	25 September: William Morris Hughes born at Pimlico, London.
1868–74	6–12	Lives in Llandudno, Wales with aunt, educated at local grammar school.
1874–84	12–22	Pupil then pupil-teacher at St Stephen's Grammar School, Pimlico, London. 1879: Australian frozen meat on sale in London.
1884	22	October: migrates to Brisbane, Queensland, Australia.

YEAR	HISTORY	CULTURE
1862	US Civil War: Lincoln's 'Emancipation Proclamation' frees all slaves in secessionist states from 1 January 1863. Otto von Bismarck becomes Prussian Prime Minister.	Ivan Turgenev, *Fathers and Sons*. Victor Hugo, *Les Misérables*. English cricket team's first Australia tour.
1868–74	1869: Suez Canal opens. 1871: Franco-Prussian War; labour unions legalised in Britain. 1872: Three Emperors' League (Germany, Russia, Austria-Hungary) established in Berlin.	1868: Louisa May Alcott, *Little Women*. Wilkie Collins, *The Moonstone*. 1869: Richard Wagner, *Rheingold*. 1873: Leo Tolstoy, *Anna Karenina*.
1874–84	1876: New Ottoman constitution proclaimed. 1878: Congress of Berlin discusses Eastern Question. 1881: First Boer War. 1882: Triple Alliance between Italy, Germany and Austria-Hungary.	1876: First complete performance of Wagner's *Ring Cycle* at Bayreuth. 1880: Fyodor Dostoevsky, *The Brothers Karamazov*. Auguste Rodin, *The Thinker*.
1884	Germans occupy South-West Africa. Berlin Conference of 14 nations on African affairs. Gold discovered in Transvaal.	Mark Twain, *Huckleberry Finn*. *Oxford English Dictionary* begins publication (-1928). Georges-Pierre Seurat, *Une Baignade à Asnières*.

YEAR	AGE	THE LIFE AND THE LAND
1884–6	22–4	Itinerant worker in outback Queensland and New South Wales.
1886	24	Arrives in Sydney as coastal ship's cook, lives in Surry Hills area, continues to do odd jobs.
1890	28	Moves to Balmain with landlord's daughter Elizabeth Cutts as common-law wife, rents shop where ekes out living mending umbrellas and locks and selling political pamphlets.
1891	29	Joins Single Tax League.
1892	30	Joins Socialist League, Labor Electoral League.

YEAR	HISTORY	CULTURE
1884–6	1885: General Gordon killed in fall of Khartoum to Mahdi. The Congo becomes personal possession of King Léopold II of Belgium. Germany annexes Tanganyika and Zanzibar.	1885: Guy de Maupassant, *Bel Ami*. H Rider Haggard, *King Solomon's Mines*. Gilbert and Sullivan, *The Mikado*.
1886	First Indian National Congress meets. Canadian-Pacific Railway completed.	Robert Louis Stevenson, *Dr Jekyll and Mr Hyde*. Frances Hodgson Burnett, *Little Lord Fauntleroy*. Karl Marx, *Das Kapital* published in English. Auguste Rodin, *The Kiss*.
1890	Bismarck dismissed by Wilhelm II. Britain exchanges Heligoland with Germany for Zanzibar and Pemba. First general election in Japan. Global influenza epidemics.	Oscar Wilde, *The Picture of Dorian Gray*. Pietro Mascagni, *Cavelleria Rusticana*. First moving picture shows in New York.
1891	Triple Alliance (Austria-Hungary, Germany, Italy) renewed for 12 years. Franco-Russian entente.	Thomas Hardy, *Tess of the D'Urbervilles*. Gustav Mahler, *Symphony No 1*. Henri de Toulouse-Lautrec produces first music-hall posters.
1892	Britain and Germany agree on Cameroon. Pan-Slav Conference in Cracow.	George Bernard Shaw, *Mrs Warren's Profession*. Israel Zangwill, *Children of the Ghetto*. Peter Tchaikovsky, *The Nutcracker*.

YEAR	AGE	THE LIFE AND THE LAND
1893	31	Works as organiser for Amalgamated Shearers' Union in central New South Wales.
		One of architects of 'Labor pledge', binding MPs to extra-parliamentary party's decisions.
1894	32	Wins seat of Lang, centred on Sydney docks, for Labor Electoral League.
1894–8	32–6	Active in New South Wales parliament.
1899	37	Organises Wharf Labourers' Union in Sydney as Secretary.
		Opposes Federation scheme for Australian colonies as undemocratic.
		Opposes participation in war in South Africa.

YEAR	HISTORY	CULTURE
1893	Franco-Russian alliance signed. Second Irish Home Rule Bill rejected by House of Lords. France acquires protectorate over Laos. Benz constructs his four-wheel car.	Oscar Wilde, *A Woman of No Importance.* Art Nouveau appears in Europe. Giacomo Puccini, *Manon Lescaut.*
1894	Sino-Japanese War begins: Japanese defeat Chinese at Port Arthur. Dreyfus Case begins in France.	George & Weedon Grossmith, *The Diary of a Nobody.* Anthony Hope, *The Prisoner of Zenda.*
1894–8	1895: Sino-Japanese War ends. Armenians massacred in Ottoman Empire. 1896: Kitchener begins reconquest of the Sudan. Russia and China sign Manchurian Convention. 1898: Kitchener defeats Mahdists at Omdurman. Spanish-American War: US gains Cuba, Puerto Rico, Guam and the Philippines.	1895: H G Wells, *The Time Machine.* W B Yeats, *Poems.* Peter Tchaikovsky, *Swan Lake.* 1896: Giacomo Puccini, *La Bohème.* Nobel Prizes established. 1898: Thomas Hardy, *Wessex Poems.* Henry James, *The Turn of the Screw.* Oscar Wilde, *The Ballad of Reading Gaol.*
1899	Anglo-Egyptian Sudan Convention. Outbreak of Second Boer War. First Peace Conference at the Hague. Dreyfus pardoned by presidential decree. Germany secures Baghdad railway contract.	Rudyard Kipling, *Stalky and Co.* Arthur Pinero, *Trelawny of the Wells.* Edward Elgar, *Enigma Variations.*

YEAR	AGE	THE LIFE AND THE LAND
1901	39	Wins seat of West Sydney (includes Sydney docks) for Labor in new federal Parliament.
		Supports the Immigration Restriction Act, basis of White Australia Policy.
		First advocates Compulsory Military Training as duty of every male adult citizen.
1902	40	Organises Waterside Workers' Federation as President.
1903	41	Admitted to New South Wales Bar.
1904	42	Minister for External Affairs in Watson's short-lived Labor Government.
		Appointed chairman of Royal Commission on Navigation, which reports in 1907.
		Supports Reid government's Commonwealth Conciliation and Arbitration Act, first introduced under Labor.

YEAR	HISTORY	CULTURE
1901	Queen Victoria dies: Edward VII becomes King. US President McKinley assassinated: Theodore Roosevelt sworn in. Negotiations for Anglo-German alliance end without agreement. First transatlantic radio signal transmitted.	First five Nobel Prizes awarded. Thomas Mann, *Die Buddenbrooks*. August Strindberg, *Dances of Death*. Rudyard Kipling, *Kim*. Pablo Picasso's 'Blue Period' begins (–1905).
1902	Treaty of Vereenigung ends Boer War. First meeting of Committee of Imperial Defence. Triple Alliance between Austria, Germany and Italy renewed for another six years. US acquires perpetual control over Panama Canal.	Maxim Gorki, *Lower Depths*. Anton Chekhov, *Three Sisters*. Claude Monet, *Waterloo Bridge*. Edward Elgar, *Pomp and Circumstance March No 1*.
1903	At London Congress, Russian Social Democratic Party splits into Mensheviks and Bolsheviks (led by Lenin and Trotsky). Wright Brothers' first flight.	Henry James, *The Ambassadors*. George Bernard Shaw, *Man and Superman*. Jack London, *The Call of the Wild*. Anton Bruckner, *Symphony No. 9*.
1904	Entente Cordiale settles British-French colonial differences. Outbreak of Russo-Japanese War. Roosevelt wins US Presidential election. Photoelectric cell invented.	J M Barrie, *Peter Pan*. Giacomo Puccini, *Madame Butterfly*. Thomas Hardy, *The Dynasts*. Anton Chekhov, *The Cherry Orchard*. Henri Rousseau, *The Wedding*. Sigmund Freud, *The Psychopathology of Everyday Life*.

YEAR	AGE	THE LIFE AND THE LAND
1905	43	Helps found New South Wales chapter of Australian National Defence League, in favour of compulsory military service.
1906	44	Death of common-law wife, Elizabeth Cutts, leaving him widower with six children.
1907	45	Visits England as official delegate to Imperial Shipping Conference; meets Lloyd George for first time.
		Writes first of series of weekly articles for *Daily Telegraph* (Sydney), later collected as *The Case for Labor* (1910) though series continues until 1911.

YEAR	HISTORY	CULTURE
1905	Port Arthur surrenders to Japanese.	'Les Fauves' christened by Louis Vauxcelles.
	Anglo-Japanese alliance renewed for ten years.	Picasso begins 'Pink Period'.
	'Bloody Sunday' – Russian demonstration broken-up by police. Tsar Nicholas II issues 'October Manifesto'.	E M Forster, *Where Angels Fear to Tread*.
		Edith Wharton, *House of Mirth*.
		Richard Strauss, *Salome*.
	Albert Einstein develops Special Theory of Relativity.	Claude Debussy, *La Mer*.
1906	Edward VII of Britain and Kaiser Wilhelm II of Germany meet.	John Galsworthy, *A Man of Property*.
	Britain grants self-government to Transvaal and Orange River Colonies.	O Henry, *The Four Million*.
		Andre Derain, *Port of London*.
	British ultimatum forces Turkey to cede Sinai Peninsula to Egypt.	Jules Massenet, *Ariane*.
		First jukebox invented.
1907	British and French agree Siamese independence.	Joseph Conrad, *The Secret Agent*.
	Dominion status granted to New Zealand.	Maxim Gorky, *Mother*.
		R M Rilke, *Neue Gedichte*.
	Edward VII in Rome, Paris and Marienbad, where he meets Russian Foreign Minister Izvolski.	First Cubist exhibition in Paris.
		Pablo Picasso, *Les Demoiselles D'Avignon*.
	Rasputin gains influence at court of Tsar Nicholas II.	Edvard Munch, *Amor and Psyche*.
	Peace Conference held in The Hague.	Frederick Delius, *A Village Romeo and Juliet*.

YEAR	AGE	THE LIFE AND THE LAND
1908	46	Attorney-General in first Fisher Labor Government.
		Wins generous pay award for Waterside Workers' Federation in new Federal Arbitration Court.
1909	47	Supports Deakin government's introduction of compulsory military training and plans for establishing Royal Australian Navy (both formally inaugurated by Labor in 1911).
1910	48	Attorney-General in second Fisher Labor Government.
		Fails to settle coal strike; incurs lasting hostility of Labor left.
		Marries 'second' time: Mary Campbell, grazier and flour miller's daughter from southern New South Wales.

YEAR	HISTORY	CULTURE
1908	Union of South Africa established. King Carlos I of Portugal and crown prince assassinated: Manuel II becomes King. Ferdinand I declares Bulgaria's independence: assumes title of Tsar.	Colette, *La Retraite Sentimentale.* E M Forster, *A Room with a View.* Kenneth Grahame, *The Wind in the Willows.* Marc Chagall, *Nu Rouge.* Bela Bartok, *String Quartet No.1.* Edward Elgar, *Symphony No. 1 in A-Flat.*
1909	King Edward VII makes State visits to Berlin, Rome. Anglo-German discussions on control of Baghdad railway. Kamil Pasha, Grand Vizier of Turkey, forced to resign by Turkish nationalists. Plastic (Bakelite) invented.	H G Wells, *Tono-Bungay* Marinetti publishes *First Futurist Manifesto.* Richard Strauss, *Elektra.* Frederick Delius, *A Mass of Life.* Henri Matisse, *The Dance.* Vasily Kandinksy paints first abstract paintings.
1910	King Edward VII dies; succeeded by George V. Egyptian Premier Butros Ghali assassinated. South Africa becomes Dominion within British Empire; Louis Botha Premier. Portugal proclaimed republic. Marie Curie publishes *Treatise on Radiography.*	E M Forster, *Howard's End.* H G Wells, *The History of Mr. Polly.* Karl May, *Winnetou.* Fernand Leger, *Nues dans le foret.* Amedeo Modigliani, *The Cellist.* Edward Elgar, *Concerto for Violin in B Minor, Op. 61.* Giacomo Puccini, *La Fanciulla del West.* R Vaughan Williams, *Sea Symphony.*

YEAR	AGE	THE LIFE AND THE LAND
1911	49	Sponsors failed referendum on federal control of trade and commerce.
1913	51	Trade and commerce referendum fails second time.
1914	52	General election returns Labor to office a month into War; Hughes becomes Attorney-General and Deputy Leader.
		Introduces War Precautions Act and Trading with Enemy Act.
1915	53	Introduces War Census Act.
		Forms Australian Metals Exchange after cleansing industry of German interests.
		27 October: becomes Prime Minister on Fisher's retirement from politics.

YEAR	HISTORY	CULTURE
1911	German gunboat *Panther* arrival in Agadir triggers international crisis. Peter Stolypyn, Russian Premier, assassinated.	Max Beerbohm, *Zuleika Dobson.* D H Lawrence, *The White Peacock.*
1913	Bulgarians renew Turkish War. King George I of Greece assassinated, succeeded by Constantine I. Second Balkan War breaks out. US Federal Reserve System established.	D H Lawrence, *Sons and Lovers.* Thomas Mann, *Death in Venice.* 'Armory Show' introduces cubism and post-impressionism to New York. Grand Central Station in New York completed.
1914	Archduke Franz Ferdinand of Austria-Hungary and wife assassinated in Sarajevo. First World War begins: Battles of Mons, the Marne, First Ypres, Tannenberg and Masurian Lakes.	James Joyce, *Dubliners.* Theodore Dreiser, *The Titan.* Gustav Holst, *The Planets.* Henri Matisse, *The Red Studio.* Georges Braque, *Music.* Film: Charlie Chaplin in *Making a Living.*
1915	First World War: Battles of Neuve Chapelle and Loos; 'Shells Scandal'; Gallipoli landings. Germans sink British liner *Lusitania,* killing 1,198.	Joseph Conrad, *Victory.* John Buchan, *The Thirty-Nine Steps.* Ezra Pound, *Cathay.* Film: *The Birth of a Nation.*

YEAR	AGE	THE LIFE AND THE LAND
1916	54	Establishes Advisory Council on Science and Industry, predecessor of Commonwealth Scientific and Industrial Organisation.
		Travels to Britain via United States, where first meets Woodrow Wilson, and Canada; speech tour of Britain attracts great interest as advocates all-out economic warfare; speeches published as *'The Day'- and After*.
		Attends Allied Economic Conference in Paris.
		Purchases 16 old steamers to form basis of Commonwealth Shipping Line.
		Negotiates grain and metals sales to Britain.
		Sworn member of Privy Councils of both Canada and United Kingdom.
		Loses first Conscription referendum.
		Leaves Australian Labor Party but remains Prime Minister at head of conservative coalition.
1917	55	Wins federal election at head of 'win-the-war' conservative coalition; moves to seat of Bendigo in rural Victoria.
		Loses second Conscription referendum by greater margin than first.

YEAR	HISTORY	CULTURE
1916	First World War.	James Joyce, *Portrait of an Artist as a Young Man.*
	Allies evacuate Gallipoli.	
	Western Front:	Vicente Blasco Ibanez, *The Four Horsemen of the Apocalypse.*
	Battles of Verdun, the Somme, Jutland.	Henri Matisse, *The Three Sisters.*
	US President Woodrow Wilson re-elected.	Claude Monet, *Waterlilies.*
	Wilson issues Peace Note to belligerents in European war.	'Dada' movement produces iconoclastic 'anti-art'.
	David Lloyd George becomes Prime Minister.	Film: *Intolerance.*
1917	First World War.	T S Eliot, *Prufrock and Other Observations.*
	Battle of Passchendaele (Third Ypres).	Piet Mondrian launches *De Stijl* magazine in Holland.
	US declares war on Germany.	Picasso designs 'surrealist' costumes and set for Satie's *Parade.*
	February Revolution in Russia.	
	Balfour Declaration favouring establishment of national home for Jewish People in Palestine.	Hans Pfitzner, *Palestrina.*
		Sergei Prokofiev, *Classical Symphony.*
		Film: *Easy Street.*

YEAR	AGE	THE LIFE AND THE LAND
1918	56	Visits United States en route to Britain, confers with Woodrow Wilson; announces need for 'Monroe Doctrine for Pacific' in speech in New York.
		Attends Imperial War Cabinet and Conference in London; sells Australian metals, wheat, butter, meat and other products to Britain.
		Unsuccessfully opposes use of Wilson's Fourteen Points as basis for Armistice, subsequent peace proposals.
1919	57	Attends Paris Peace Conference: Deputy Chairman of Reparations Commission, clashes with Wilson over proposed annexation of German New Guinea, agrees to compromise with 'C' class Mandate; defeats Japanese racial equality clause proposal for League of Nations Charter, protects White Australia policy; wins share of Nauru phosphate deposits; fails to win full reparations.
		Returns to Australia.
		Conservative coalition returned to office at general election.
		Takes silk as King's Counsel.

YEAR	HISTORY	CULTURE
1918	First World War.	Alexander Blok, *The Twelve*.
	Peace Treaty of Brest-Litovsk between Russia and Central Powers.	Gerald Manley Hopkins, *Poems*.
		Luigi Pirandello, *Six Characters in Search of an Author*.
	German Spring offensives on Western Front fail.	Bela Bartok, *Bluebeard's Castle*.
		Giacomo Puccini, *Il Trittico*.
	Romania signs Peace of Bucharest with Germany, Austria-Hungary.	Gustav Cassel, *Theory of Social Economy*.
	Ex-Tsar Nicholas II and family executed.	Oskar Kokoshka, *Friends* and *Saxonian Landscape*.
	Allied offensives on Western Front have German army in full retreat.	Edvard Munch, *Bathing Man*.
	Armistice signed between Allies, Germany; German Fleet surrenders.	
	Kaiser Wilhelm II of Germany abdicates.	
	Women over 30 get right to vote in Britain.	
1919	Communist Revolt in Berlin.	Bauhaus movement founded by Walter Gropius.
	Paris Peace Conference adopts principle of founding League of Nations.	Thomas Hardy, *Collected Poems*.
	Benito Mussolini founds Fascist movement in Italy.	George Bernard Shaw, *Heartbreak House*.
	Treaty of Versailles signed.	Film: *The Cabinet of Dr Caligari*.
	Irish War of Independence begins.	
	US Senate votes against ratification of Versailles Treaty, leaving US outside League of Nations.	

YEAR	AGE	THE LIFE AND THE LAND
1920	58	Forms Commonwealth Oil Refineries Pty Ltd.
		Admirers in Britain, Australia present him with £25,000 cheque as reward for War work.
1921	59	Attends Imperial Conference in London: helps defeat proposals for Imperial Federation, defends Anglo-Japanese Treaty, lays basis for Washington Conference of 1921–2, advocates improved Imperial air and wireless communications.
1922	60	Mary Hughes created Dame in New Year's Honours List.
		Organises government involvement in Amalgamated Wireless (Australasia) Ltd, becomes director.
		Critical of British government's conduct in Chanak Crisis.
		Moves seat to North Sydney at federal elections; Country Party under Earle Page gain balance of power.

YEAR	HISTORY	CULTURE
1920	League of Nations comes into existence.	F Scott Fitzgerald, *This Side of Paradise*.
	Bolsheviks win Russian Civil War.	Katherine Mansfield, *Bliss*.
	Adolf Hitler announces 25-point programme in Munich.	Rambert School of Ballet formed.
	US Constitutional Amendments: 18th (Prohibition) goes into effect, 19th gives women right to vote.	Maurice Ravel, *La Valse*.
1921	Irish Free State established.	Aldous Huxley, *Chrome Yellow*.
	Peace Treaty signed between Russia and Germany.	D H Lawrence, *Women in Love*.
	State of Emergency proclaimed in Germany in face of economic crisis.	Sergei Prokofiev, *The Love for Three Oranges*.
	Washington Naval Treaty signed.	
1922	Britain recognises Kingdom of Egypt under Fuad I.	T S Eliot, *The Waste Land*.
	Election in Irish Free State gives majority to Pro-Treaty candidates. IRA takes large areas under control.	James Joyce, *Ulysses*.
		F Scott Fitzgerald, *The Beautiful and Damned*.
	League of Nations Council approves British Mandate in Palestine.	British Broadcasting Company (later Corporation) (BBC) founded: first radio broadcasts.

YEAR	AGE	THE LIFE AND THE LAND
1923	61	Country Party, some Nationalists oust him as Prime Minister in favour of S M Bruce; Bruce-Page Coalition Government formed.
1924	62	Unsuccessful lecture tour of United States.
1925– 9	63–7	Backbench critic of Bruce-Page Government, particularly sale of Commonwealth Shipping Line 1927, plans to end deferral involvement in industrial arbitration.

YEAR	HISTORY	CULTURE
1923	Peace is signed at Lausanne. French, Belgian troops occupy the Ruhr when Germany fails to make reparation payments. USSR formally comes into existence. State of Emergency declared in Germany. British Mandate in Palestine begins. Adolf Hitler's *coup d'état* (The Beer Hall Putsch) fails.	P G Wodehouse, *The Inimitable Jeeves*. George Gershwin, *Rhapsody in Blue*. Bela Bartok, *Dance Suite*. BBC listings magazine *Radio Times* first published.
1924	Lenin dies. Dawes Plan published. Greece proclaimed republic.	Noel Coward, *The Vortex*. E M Forster, *A Passage to India*. Thomas Mann, *The Magic Mountain*. George Bernard Shaw, *St Joan*.
1925–9	1925: Locarno Treaty signed in London. 1926: Germany admitted into League of Nations. 1928: Kellogg-Briand Pact outlawing war, providing for peaceful settlement of disputes signed. German Plebiscite against building new battleships fails. Alexander Fleming discovers Penicillin.	1925: Franz Kafka, *The Trial*. Virginia Woolf, *Mrs Dalloway*. Film: *Battleship Potemkin*. 1926: Sean O'Casey, *The Plough and The Stars*. Giacomo Puccini, *Turandot*. 1927: Marcel Proust, *Le Temps retrouve*. Virginia Woolf, *To the Lighthouse*. 1928: D H Lawrence, *Lady Chatterley's Lover*. George Gershwin, *An American in Paris*. Kurt Weill, *The Three Penny Opera*.

YEAR	AGE	THE LIFE AND THE LAND
1929	67	Publishes *The Splendid Adventure*.
		Secret talks with Labor Shadow Treasurer Ted Theodore on proto-Keynesian solutions to combat early effects of Great Depression.
		Crosses floor over Arbitration reforms, thereby orchestrates defeat of Bruce-Page Government.
1930	68	Establishes short-lived Australian Party.
1931	69	Supports Lyons' United Australia Party conservative government.

YEAR	HISTORY	CULTURE
1929	King Alexander I establishes dictatorship Yugoslavia. Fascists win single-party elections in Italy. Germany accepts Young Plan at Reparations Conference in the Hague – Allies agree to evacuate the Rhineland. Arabs attack Jews in Palestine following dispute over Jewish use of Western Wall. Wall Street crashes.	Jean Cocteau, *Les Enfants Terribles*. Ernest Hemingway, *A Farewell to Arms*. Erich Maria Remarque, *All Quiet on the Western Front*. Marc Chagall, *Love Idyll*. Piet Mondrian, *Composition with Yellow and Blue*. Museum of Modern Art New York opens. Noel Coward, *Bittersweet*.
1930	United Kingdom, France, Italy, Japan and US sign London Naval Treaty regulating naval expansion. British Imperial Conference held in London. Acrylic plastics invented.	T S Eliot, *Ash Wednesday*. W H Auden, *Poems*. Bela Bartok, *Cantata Profana*. Igor Stravinsky, *Symphony of Psalms*. Alfred Adler, *The inferiority complex*. Film: *All Quiet on the Western Front*.
1931	Bankruptcy of Austria's Credit-Anstalt begins financial collapse of Central Europe. National Government formed in Great Britain. Nazi leader Adolf Hitler and Alfred Hugenberg of German National Party agree to co-operate.	William Faulkner, *Sanctuary*. Robert Frost, *Collected Poems*. Salvador Dali, *The Persistence of Memory*. Max Beckmann, *Still Life with Studio Window*. Architecture: Empire State Building New York.

YEAR	AGE	THE LIFE AND THE LAND
1932	70	Delegate to General Assembly of League of Nations.
1933	71	Establishes Defence of Australia League.
1934	72	Publishes *The Price of Peace* arguing for rearmament. Appointed Minister for Health and Repatriation, Vice-President of Executive Council in second Lyons Government.
1935	73	Publishes *Australia and War To-day*, arguing against sanctions being applied to Italy over invasion of Abyssinia, in favour of rearmament; stands down from Cabinet temporarily for disagreeing with its foreign policy.

YEAR	HISTORY	CULTURE
1932	Germany withdraws temporarily from Geneva Disarmament Conference, demanding permission for armaments equal to other powers. Britain, France, Germany and Italy make 'No Force Declaration', renouncing use of force for settling differences.	Aldous Huxley, *Brave New World*. Pablo Picasso, *Head of a Woman*. Samuel Barber, *Overture to School for Scandal*. Sergei Prokofiev, *Piano Concerto No.5 in G major Op. 55*
1933	Adolf Hitler appointed Chancellor of Germany. Germany withdraws from League of Nations, Disarmament Conference.	George Orwell, *Down and Out in Paris and London*. Films: *Duck Soup. King Kong. Queen Christina*.
1934	Germany, 'Night of the Long Knives'. Hitler becomes *Führer*. USSR admitted to League of Nations.	Robert Graves, *I, Claudius*. Sergei Rakhmaninov, *Rhapsody on a theme of Paganini*. Jean Cocteau, *La Machine Infernale*. Film: *David Copperfield*.
1935	Prime Ministers of Italy, France and Britain issue protest at German rearmament, agree to act together against Germany. Hoare-Laval Pact. Hitler announces anti-Jewish 'Nuremberg Laws'; Swastika becomes Germany's official flag. League of Nations imposes sanctions against Italy following invasion of Abyssinia.	George Gershwin, *Porgy and Bess*. Richard Strauss, *Die Schweigsame Frau*. T S Eliot, *Murder in the Cathedral*. Ivy Compton-Burnett, *A House and its Head*. Films: *The 39 Steps. Top Hat*.

YEAR	AGE	THE LIFE AND THE LAND
1937	75	Unmarried 22-year-old daughter Helen dies in London of complications following Caesarian birth.
		Appointed Minister for External Affairs.
1938	76	Clashes with German Consul in Australia over proposed return of New Guinea to Germany; sceptical about Munich Agreement.
		Placed in charge of recruitment for expanded militia.
1939	77	Contests leadership of United Australia Party (UAP) on Lyons' death, comes second to Robert Menzies.
		Appointed Attorney-General and Minster for Industry.

YEAR	HISTORY	CULTURE
1937	UK Royal Commission on Palestine recommends partition into British and Arab areas and Jewish state. Italy joins German-Japanese Anti-Comintern Pact.	Jean-Paul Sartre, *Nausea*. John Steinbeck, *Of Mice and Men*. Films: *Snow White and the Seven Dwarfs. A Star is Born. La Grande Illusion*.
1938	German troops enter Austria: declared part of German Reich. Munich Agreement hands Sudetenland to Germany. Kristallnacht in Germany: Jewish houses, synagogues and schools burnt for a week. Nuclear fission discovered in Germany.	Graham Greene, *Brighton Rock*. Evelyn Waugh, *Scoop*. Ballpoint pen patented in Hungary. *Picture Post* founded in Britain. Films: *Pygmalion, Alexander Nevsky*.
1939	Germans troops enter Prague. Italy invades Albania. Pact of Steel signed by Hitler and Mussolini. Nazi-Soviet Pact agrees no fighting, partition of Poland: Japanese withdraw from Anti-Comintern Pact in protest. Germany invades Poland: Britain and France declare war.	James Joyce, *Finnegan's Wake*. Thomas Mann, *Lotte in Weimar*. John Steinbeck, *The Grapes of Wrath*. Films: *Gone with the Wind. Goodbye Mr Chips. The Wizard of Oz*.

YEAR	AGE	THE LIFE AND THE LAND
1940	78	Re-appointed Attorney-General after general election, also Minister for Navy.
1941	79	Becomes leader of UAP when Curtin Labor Government assumes office.
		Appointed to Advisory War Council.
		Appointed Companion of Honour.
1943	81	Becomes Deputy Leader of UAP when Menzies resumes leadership.

YEAR	HISTORY	CULTURE
1940	Second World War.	Wassily Kandinsky, *Sky Blue*.
	Norwegian campaign failure causes Chamberlain to resign, Churchill becomes Prime Minister.	Graham Greene, *The Power and the Glory*.
		Ernest Hemingway, *For Whom the Bell Tolls*.
	Germany invades Holland, Belgium, Luxembourg.	Eugene O'Neill, *Long Day's Journey into Night*.
	Italy declares war on France and Britain.	
	Battle of Britain.	
	France divides into German-occupied north, Vichy south.	
1941	Second World War.	Bertold Brecht, *Mother Courage and Her Children*.
	Germany invades USSR	Noel Coward, *Blithe Spirit*.
	Japanese troops occupy Indochina.	British communist paper, *The Daily Worker*, suppressed.
	Germany besieges Leningrad and Moscow.	Films: *Citizen Kane. Dumbo. The Maltese Falcon*.
	Japan attacks Pearl Harbor,	
	invades Philippines.	
	Germany and Italy declare war on US.	
	Atomic bomb development begins in US	
1943	Second World War.	Jean-Paul Sartre, *Being and Nothingness*.
	Allied landings in French North Africa.	Richard Rogers and Oscar Hammerstein, *Oklahoma!*
	Italian King dismisses Mussolini: Italy surrenders unconditionally.	Jean-Paul Sartre, *The Flies*.
	Tehran Conference: Churchill, Roosevelt and Stalin meet.	*Frankfurter Zeitung* ordered to cease publication.

YEAR	AGE	THE LIFE AND THE LAND
1944	82	Expelled from UAP when refuses to resign from Advisory War Council, but joins Menzies' new Liberal Party.
1947	85	Publishes memoir, *Crusts and Crusades*.
1949	87	Elected for new federal seat of Bradfield (takes in part of old North Sydney constituency).
1950	88	Publishes second volume of memoirs, *Policies and Potentates*.

YEAR	HISTORY	CULTURE
1944	British and US forces in Italy liberate Rome.	Carl Jung, *Psychology and Religion.*
	D-Day landings in France.	Michael Tippett, *A Child of Our Time.*
	Free French enter Paris.	
	US President Franklin Roosevelt wins fourth term.	T S Eliot, *Four Quartets.*
	German counter-offensive in the Ardennes.	Terrence Rattigan, *The Winslow Boy.*
		Tennessee Williams, *The Glass Menagerie.*
1947	Moscow Conference fails over problem of Germany.	Albert Camus, *The Plague.*
	Indian Independence and Partition.	Tennessee Williams, *A Streetcar Named Desire.*
	New Japanese constitution renounces use of war.	Le Corbusier, Unité d'Habitation Marseille, France.
1949	North Atlantic Treaty Organisation (NATO) founded.	Simone de Beauvoir, *The Second Sex.*
	Berlin blockade lifted.	Jacob Epstein, *Lazarus.*
	West Germany comes into being.	Richard Rogers and Oscar Hammerstein, *South Pacific.*
	Mao Zedong establishes People's Republic of China.	George Orwell, *Nineteen Eighty-Four.*
	Legislated Apartheid begins in South Africa.	Arthur Miller, *Death of a Salesman.*
	USSR tests first atomic bomb.	
1950	Korean War begins.	Pablo Neruda, *General Song.*
	USSR and China sign 30-year Treaty of Friendship.	Ezra Pound, *Seventy Cantos.*
	West Germany joins Council of Europe.	Films: *Orphée. Rashomon. Sunset Boulevard.*

YEAR	AGE	THE LIFE AND THE LAND
1952	90	28 October: dies at home in Lindfield, Sydney; given state funeral.

YEAR	HISTORY	CULTURE
1952	King George VI dies: succeeded by Elizabeth II. Mau-Mau Rising in Kenya. Electric power produced from atomic energy in US.	Henry Moore, *King and Queen*. Dylan Thomas, *Collected Poems*. Evelyn Waugh, *Men at Arms*. Agatha Christie, *The Mousetrap*.

Further Reading

The official biography of William Morris Hughes by L F Fitzhardinge (*That Fiery Particle*, Vol. I, 1964; and *The Little Digger*, Vol. II, 1979) is an impressive and thorough piece of work and the place to start exploring Hughes's life and career. Other useful works on him are Malcolm Booker's *The Great Professional* (1980), which concentrates on his political methods and achievements; Donald Horne's *Billy Hughes* (1979 and 2000), which looks at his rhetoric; and Aneurin Hughes, *Billy Hughes* (2005), which, though uneven in quality, sheds important new light on his family life. Hughes's own memoirs, *The Splendid Adventure* (1929), *Crusts and Crusades* (1947) and *Policies and Potentates* (1950) are colourful and revealing, but must be read with caution.

The early years of the Labor Party in Australia can be followed in Ray Markey, *The Making of the Labor Party in New South Wales, 1880–1900* (1988) and Ross McMullin, *The Light on the Hill* (1991). Federal politics are thoroughly treated in Gavin Souter's *Acts of Parliament* (1988) and the wider Australian social context in his *Lion and Kangaroo: Australia 1901–1919* (1976).

The best general introduction to the military side of

Australia's War is the relevant section of Jeffrey Grey's *A Military History of Australia* (3rd edn, 2008). Also important here are John Robertson's *Anzac and Empire* (1990) and E M Andrews's *The Anzac Illusion* (1993). For the home front, the most comprehensive and illuminating account is still Ernest Scott's *Australia during the War* (1936). This should be supplemented by Michael McKernan, *The Australian People and the Great War* (1980); Joan Beaumont, ed., *Australia's War, 1914–18* (1995); and L L Robson's collection of documents, *Australia and the Great War* (1969). The battle over conscription still awaits its historian, but see L C Jauncey, *Conscription in Australia* (1935), and J M Main, ed., *Conscription: the Australian Debate* (1970). The best biographies of Hughes's main anti-conscription protagonist are B A Santamaria, *Daniel Mannix* (1984), and Michael Gilchrist, *Daniel Mannix* (2004). Valuable regional studies are Marilyn Lake's *A Divided Society* (1975) on Tasmania, John McQuilton's *Rural Australia and the Great War* (2001), Ray Evans' *Loyalty and Disloyalty* (1987) on Queensland, and Bobbie Oliver's *War and Peace in Western Australia* (1995). A stimulating corrective to much labour mythologising is John Hirst's chapter on 'Labor and the Great War' in Robert Manne, ed., *The Australian Century* (1999). On the broader labour movement at war, see Frank Cain, *The Wobblies at War* (1993), and the two studies by Ian Turner, *Industrial Labour and Politics* (1965) and *Sydney's Burning* (1967).

Australia's wartime commodity diplomacy is covered well in Kosmas Tsokhas, *Markets, Money and Empire* (1990); Peter Cochrane, *Industrialization and Dependence* (1980); and, in comparative context, in Avner Offer, *The First World War: An Agrarian Interpretation* (1989). Australia's war finances and economy are discussed best in D B Copland's sub-chapter in

J Holland Rose *et al.*, *The Cambridge History of the British Empire, Vol. VII, Pt I, Australia* (1933).

On Australian defence and foreign policy in Hughes's period, Neville Meaney's two volumes, *The Search for Security in the Pacific* (1976) and *Australia and World Crisis* (2009) are indispensable. See also the two documentary collections: Gordon Greenwood and Charles Grimshaw, eds, *Documents on Australian International Affairs, 1901–1918* (1977) and Neville Meaney, ed., *Australia and the World* (1985).

On Hughes at Versailles, W J Hudson, *Billy Hughes in Paris* (1978) is the most helpful introduction, and it usefully includes a collection of key documents. Another significant study is Peter Spartalis, *The Diplomatic Battles of Billy Hughes* (1983). On the views of the rest of the Australian delegation, see Sir Robert Garran's memoir, *Prosper the Commonwealth* (1958) and Warren G Osmond's *Frederic Eggleston* (1985). David Low, *The Billy Book* (1918), published on the eve of the Conference, is the celebrated cartoonist's popular impression of Hughes as innocent abroad. Paul Bartrop, *Bolt from the Blue* (2002), is revealing about Australia and Chanak.

The most accessible introduction to the Peace Conference is Margaret MacMillan's *Peacemakers* (2002). The long-term Imperial perspective can be traced in John Darwin's *The Imperial Project* (2010).

The following websites contain information on Hughes, including contemporary posters, photographs and film footage:

www.oph.gov.au: Old Parliament House, Canberra, 'Billy Hughes at War' virtual exhibition.

www.ww1westernfront.gov.au: Department of Veterans' Affairs 'Western Front of World War One'.

www.awm.gov.au: Australian War Memorial, Canberra.

www.primeministers.naa.gov.au: National Archives of
   Australia.

www.australiansatwork.com.au: Film Australia: World War
   One and the Conscription Referenda (1916, 1917).

www.abc.net.au/rn/bigidea/patriots: ABC Radio National:
   'Patriots three' by Jill Kitson.

Select Bibliography

Primary sources
Official records
Cables from Hughes' visit abroad, CP 290/3
Cables exchanged between Hughes and Watt, 1918–20, CP
    360/8, 9, 11, 13

Newspapers and magazines
Argus
Bulletin
Daily Telegraph (Sydney)
Herald (Melbourne)
The Times
Sydney Morning Herald

Private papers
Earl Balfour Papers, British Library, London.
Sir Joseph Cook Collection, National Library of Australia,
    Canberra.
W M Hughes Collection, National Library of Australia,
    Canberra.

Sir Robert Garran Papers, National Library of Australia, Canberra.

David Lloyd George Papers, House of Lords Library, London.

Sir John G Latham Collection, National Library of Australia, Canberra.

Sir Keith Murdoch Papers, National Library of Australia, Canberra.

Lord Novar Papers, National Library of Australia, Canberra.

Sir George Pearce Papers, Australian War Memorial, Canberra

Official printed sources

Commonwealth of Australia, Parliamentary Debates

New South Wales, Parliamentary Debates

United States Department of State, *Foreign Relations of the United States: Papers Relating to the Paris Peace Conference* 1919, 13 Vols (State Department, Washington, DC: 1942–7).

Unofficial printed sources including memoirs

Burnett, P M, ed. *Reparations at the Peace Conference*, 2 Vols (Columbia University Press, New York: 1940).

Garran, Robert. *Prosper the Commonwealth* (Angus & Robertson, Sydney: 1958).

House, E M and C Seymour, eds. *What Really Happened at Paris: The Story of the Peace Conference* (C. Scribner's Sons, New York: 1921).

Hughes, W M. *Australia and War To-day: The Price of Peace* (Angus & Robertson, Sydney: 1935).

_____. *Crusts and Crusades: Tales of Bygone Days* (Angus & Robertson, Sydney: 1947).

_____. *The Case for Labor* (The Worker Trustees, Sydney: 1910).

_____. *'The Day' – and after* (Cassell, London: 1916).

_____. *Policies and Potentates* (Angus & Robertson, Sydney: 1950).

_____. *The Price of Peace* (Defense of Australia League, Sydney: 1934).

_____. *The Splendid Adventure: A Review of Empire Relations* (Ernest Benn, London: 1929).

Lloyd George, David. *The Truth about the Peace Treaties*, Vol. 1 (Gollancz, London: 1938).

Low, David. *The Billy Book: Hughes Abroad* (NSW Bookstall Co, Sydney: 1918).

Miller, David Hunter. *My Diary at the Conference of Paris with Documents*, Vol. VII (Appeal Printing Company, New York: 1924).

Nicolson, Harold. *Peacemaking 1919* (Constable, London: 1933).

Secondary sources

Andrews, Eric. *The Anzac Illusion: Anglo-Australian Relations during World War I* (Cambridge University Press, Melbourne: 1993).

_____. *Isolationism and Appeasement in Australia: Reactions to the European Crises, 1935–1939* (Australian National University Press, Canberra: 1970).

Bartrop, Paul R. *Bolt from the Blue: Australia, Britain and the Chanak Crisis* (Halstead Press, Sydney: 2002).

Bonsal, Stephen. *Suitors and Suppliants* (Prentice-Hall, New York: 1946).

Brady, E J. *Doctor Mannix: Archbishop of Melbourne* (Library of National Biography, Melbourne: 1934).

Brennan, Niall. *Dr Mannix* (Angus & Robertson, London: 1965).

Browne, Frank. *They Called Him Billy* (Peter Hudson, Sydney: 1946).

Booker, Malcolm. *The Great Professional: A Study of W. M. Hughes* (McGraw-Hill, Sydney: 1980).

Cochrane, Peter. *Industrialization and Dependence: Australia's Road to Economic Development 1870–1939* (University of Queensland Press, Brisbane: 1980).

Fitzhardinge, L F. *A Political Biography of William Morris Hughes: Vol. 1 That Fiery Particle 1862–1914* and *Vol. 2 The Little Digger 1914–1952* (Angus & Robertson, Sydney: 1964 & 1979).

Gilchrist, Michael. *Daniel Mannix: Wit and Wisdom* (Freedom Publishing, Melbourne: 2004).

Grey, Jeffrey. *A Military History of Australia* (Cambridge University Press, Melbourne: 3rd edition, 2008).

Haig-Muir, Marnie. 'The Economy at War', Ch. 4 in Joan Beaumont, ed., *Australia's War* (Allen & Unwin, Sydney: 1995).

Hirst, John. 'Labor and the Great War' in Robert Manne, ed., *The Australian Century: Political Struggle in the Building of a Nation* (Text, Melbourne: 1999).

Horne, Donald. *Billy Hughes* (Black Inc, Melbourne: 2000, first pub. 1979).

Hudson, W J. *Billy Hughes in Paris: The Birth of Australian Diplomacy* (Nelson, Melbourne: 1978).

Hughes, Aneurin. *Billy Hughes: Prime Minister and Controversial Founding Father of the Australian Labor Party* (Wiley, Brisbane: 2005).

Jauncey, L C. *The Story of Conscription in Australia* (Macmillan, Melbourne: 1968, first pub. 1935).

Lowe, David. 'Australia in the World', Ch. 5 in Joan Beaumont, ed., *Australia's War* (Allen & Unwin, Sydney: 1995).

Markey, Raymond. *The Making of the Labor Party in New South Wales, 1880–1900* (University of New South Wales Press, Sydney: 1988).

McKernan, Michael. *The Australian People and the Great War* (Nelson, Melbourne: 1980).

Meaney, Neville. *A History of Australian Defence and Foreign Policy 1901–23: Vol. 1 The Search for Security in the Pacific 1901–14* and *Vol. 2 Australia and World Crisis, 1914–1923* (Sydney University Press, Sydney: 1976 & 2009).

MacMillan, Margaret. *Peacemakers: The Peace Conference of 1919 and Its Attempt to End War* (John Murray, London: 2001).

Nish, Ian. *Alliance in Decline: A Study in Anglo-Japanese Relations, 1908–23* (Athlone Press, London: 1972).

Offer, Avner. *The First World War: An Agrarian Interpretation* (Oxford University Press, Oxford: 1989).

Perry, F W. *The Commonwealth Armies: Manpower and Organisation in Two World Wars* (Manchester University Press, Manchester: 1988).

Santamaria, B A. *Daniel Mannix: The Quality of Leadership* (Melbourne University Press, Melbourne: 1984).

Sawer, Geoffrey. *Australian Federal Politics and Law, 1901–1929* (Melbourne University Press, Melbourne: 1956).

Spartalis, Peter. *The Diplomatic Battles of Billy Hughes* (Hale & Iremonger, Sydney: 1983).

Scott, Ernest. *Australia During the War: The Official History of Australia in the War of 1914–1918*, Vol. XI (Angus & Robertson, Sydney: 1936).

Souter, Gavin. *Acts of Parliament: A Narrative History of Australia's Federal Legislature* (Melbourne University Press, Melbourne: 1988).

_____. *Lion and Kangaroo. Australia: 1901–1919. The Rise of a Nation* (Fontana, Sydney: 1976).

Tsokhas, Kosmas. *Markets, Money and Empire: The Political Economy of the Australian Wool Industry* (Melbourne University Press, Melbourne: 1990).

Turner, Ian. *Industrial Labour and Politics: The Dynamics of the Labour Movement in Australia, 1900–1921* (Australian National University Press, Canberra: 1965).

_____. *Sydney's Burning* (Heinemann, Melbourne: 1967).

White, Les. *Wool in Wartime: A Study in Colonialism* (APCOL, Sydney: 1981).

Whyte, W Farmer. *William Morris Hughes* (Angus & Robertson, Sydney: 1957.

Picture Sources

The author and publishers wish to express their thanks to the following sources of illustrative material and/or permission to reproduce it. They will make proper acknowledgements in future editions in the event that any omissions have occurred.

Topham Picturepoint.

Endpapers
The Signing of Peace in the Hall of Mirrors, Versailles, 28th June 1919 by Sir William Orpen (Imperial War Museum: akg-images)
Front row: Dr Johannes Bell (Germany) signing with Herr Hermann Müller leaning over him
Middle row (seated, left to right): General Tasker H Bliss, Col E M House, Mr Henry White, Mr Robert Lansing, President Woodrow Wilson (United States); M Georges Clemenceau (France); Mr David Lloyd George, Mr Andrew Bonar Law, Mr Arthur J Balfour, Viscount Milner, Mr G N Barnes (Great Britain); Prince Saionji (Japan)
Back row (left to right): M Eleftherios Venizelos (Greece);

Dr Afonso Costa (Portugal); Lord Riddell (British Press); Sir George E Foster (Canada); M Nikola Pašić (Serbia); M Stephen Pichon (France); Col Sir Maurice Hankey, Mr Edwin S Montagu (Great Britain); the Maharajah of Bikaner (India); Signor Vittorio Emanuele Orlando (Italy); M Paul Hymans (Belgium); General Louis Botha (South Africa); Mr W M Hughes (Australia)

Jacket images

(Front): Imperial War Museum: akg Images.
(Back): *Peace Conference at the Quai d'Orsay* by Sir William Orpen (Imperial War Museum: akg Images).
Left to right (seated): Signor Orlando (Italy); Mr Robert Lansing, President Woodrow Wilson (United States); M Georges Clemenceau (France); Mr David Lloyd George, Mr Andrew Bonar Law, Mr Arthur J Balfour (Great Britain); Left to right (standing): M Paul Hymans (Belgium); Mr Eleftherios Venizelos (Greece); The Emir Feisal (The Hashemite Kingdom); Mr W F Massey (New Zealand); General Jan Smuts (South Africa); Col E M House (United States); General Louis Botha (South Africa); Prince Saionji (Japan); Mr W M Hughes (Australia); Sir Robert Borden (Canada); Mr G N Barnes (Great Britain); M Ignacy Paderewski (Poland)

Index

Makers
of the
Modern
World

UK PUBLICATION: November 2008 to December 2010
CLASSIFICATION: Biography/History/
    International Relations
FORMAT: 198 × 128mm
EXTENT: 208pp
ILLUSTRATIONS: 6 photographs plus 4 maps
TERRITORY: world

Chronology of life in context, full index, bibliography innovative layout
with sidebars